THE ROYAL COMMISSION ON CRIMINAL JUSTICE

The Right to Silence
in Police Interrogation

A Study of Some of the Issues Underlying the Debate

by **Roger Leng**

LONDON: HMSO

CONTENTS

1. INTRODUCTION

The right to silence in police interrogation

The right to silence as presently understood is expressed in two distinct rules of law. The first is that no person, including a suspect, may be required to give information to the police in the course of a criminal investigation. Thus, a suspect under interrogation may decline to answer questions altogether, or may decline to answer particular questions or may decline to give particular pieces of information in his answers to questions. The second rule is that a person charged with a criminal offence cannot be required to give evidence in court at any stage of criminal proceedings. The present study will focus on the first rule and will seek to test some of the assumptions which apparently underlie arguments for modifying or abolishing the right.

It can be said that a suspect has a right to silence in police interrogation only to the extent that no lawful sanction may be applied to him for remaining silent. It has long been accepted that the fact that the suspect has a right to remain silent does not imply a duty on the police not to seek to persuade him to answer.[1] Indeed under the Police and Criminal Evidence Act, the police are empowered to detain a suspect where this is considered necessary in order to obtain evidence by questioning.[2] In practice this is interpreted as permitting the police to continue to question after the suspect has indicated that he does not wish to answer, and also as permitting further detention (within the time limits laid down by PACE) for the purpose of re-interview after a lapse of time. Although the effect of these rules and practices is that a suspect may be detained longer because of his silence, this is not generally considered to be a sanction which negatives the right to silence. The reasoning underlying this appears to be that all citizens may be required to submit to detention and questioning where the conditions set out in the PACE Act are fulfilled. Thus, where the silent suspect is further detained he is simply fulfilling this general social duty rather than suffering punishment for silence.

---

[1] *Rice* v *Connolly* [1966] 2 QB 414.
[2] The courts have also accepted that detention is lawful for the purpose of placing psychological pressure on the suspect, even where there is otherwise no need for detention because the suspect is willing to be interviewed elsewhere: *Holgate-Mohammed* v *Duke* [1984] 1 All ER 1054.

Also under present law the suspect who is silent in police interview, suffers no automatic legal sanction for this in the trial process. As has often been pointed out, there is nothing to stop a bench of magistrates or jury from treating silence as indicative of guilt,[3] but a jury cannot be directly invited to reach this conclusion by prosecuting counsel or the judge.[4] Arguments for modifying or abolishing the right to silence focus on this rule. Thus, in 1972 the Criminal Law Revision Committee (CLRC) recommended that the law should be amended to allow a court or jury to draw adverse inferences against an accused person if in the course of interrogation he had failed to mention any fact which he later relied upon by way of defence at committal proceedings or trial.[5] The major significance of this change would be to permit counsel and trial judges to indicate to juries what inferences might be drawn from silence, including inferences of guilt.[6] The CLRC also recommended that if their proposal were to be enacted a new caution should be adopted which would be administered before the suspect was charged or informed that he might be charged. The effect of the proposed caution would be to advise the suspect that if he intended to rely upon a defence he should mention it at that stage. He would further be warned that if he were to hold back his defence until court, it would be less likely to be believed and that this might have a bad effect on his case in general.[7]

Under the CLRCs proposals the silent suspect would risk an inference being drawn against him, not only where he raised a defence at trial, but also where he maintained his silence at trial. This follows from the CLRC's complementary proposal that it should be possible to draw inferences against an accused person who had declined to give evidence in the face of a *prima facie* case against him.[8]

Although, the reforms proposed by the CLRC relate to the law of evidence applying in criminal trials, their most significant effect would not

---

[3] The Royal Commission on Criminal Procedure (1981B), para 83.

[4] For a discussion of the scope of permissible judicial comment on the accused's silence see Easton (1991), pp. 9–17.

[5] Criminal Law Revision Committee (1972), para 32 and cl. 1 of the Draft Criminal Evidence Bill appended to the Report.

[6] Under cl 1 Draft Criminal Evidence Bill *ibid*, it would be permissible to draw inferences only where the fact relied upon at trial was one which the suspect could have been reasonably expected to mention in the cirucumstances existing at the time of the interrogation. Under cl 1, inferences from silence may also be treated: (i) as evidence, by magistrates determining whether to commit a person for trial, and by a judge determining whether there is a case to answer; (ii) as corroboration of other evidence against the accused.

[7] *Ibid* para 44.

[8] Criminal Law Revision Committee (1972), paras 108–113 and cl 5, Draft Criminal Evidence Bill appended to the Report.

be to create a new source of evidence to enhance the prospects of conviction.[9] Rather, the major impact of the reforms would be to put pressure on the accused to disclose his story at an early stage.[10] It has also been claimed that such a reform would prevent the court of trial being ambushed by a defence, heard for the first time on the day of trial.

The Royal Commission on Criminal Procedure whose Report published in 1981 laid the foundations for the Police and Criminal Evidence Act 1984, rejected the CLRC's proposals on two grounds: first, that the extra psychological pressure to raise a defence might increase the risk of innocent suspects making damaging statements; secondly, that there would be an inconsistency in principle in placing the burden of proof on the prosecution whilst allowing the prosecution to use the accused's silence under questioning as part of the prosecution case against him.[11] However, the debate about modifying or abolishing the right to silence was rekindled by the Home Secretary, Mr. Hurd in his Police Foundation speech of July 1987. Reform effectively became Government policy when the Home Secretary announced the setting up of the Home Office Working Group on the Right to Silence in May 1988, however the policy was shelved following the appointment of the Royal Commission on Criminal Procedure and pending the publication of the Commission's Report.

The remit of the Home Office Working Group was to advise on the precise form of the change in the law which would be required in order to achieve the Government's purpose in removing the protection which the law gives to the accused person who ambushes the prosecution. The Group's recommendations followed those of the CLRC and would permit the prosecution, defence and the trial judge to comment on the failure of an accused person to mention any fact which he subsequently relied upon at trial. The Working Group also favoured the introduction of a modified caution along the lines recommended by the CLRC, but to be administered on arrest, prior to interview and when charged (as the present caution), rather than only when the suspect is charged (as recommended by the CLRC). The Working Group did not follow the CLRC in recommending change to the law relating to silence in court, except that they would have permitted counsel to comment on silence in the same terms in which judges are currently permitted to comment.

---

[9] It may be doubted whether a court of jury would ever feel confident in attaching much evidential weight to silence: Ruddell (1990), pp. 53-59; Jackson (1991), and Jackson (1992).
[10] See the view of the minority of the Criminal Law Revision Committee (1972), para 52 (iv), and C.J, Miller (1973), p. 349.
[11] Royal Commission on Criminal Procedure (1981A), paras 4.50, 4.51.

Prior to the publication of the Home Office Working Group's proposals, the law on the right to silence was substantially modified in Northern Ireland by the Criminal Evidence (Northern Ireland) Order 1988. The Order was introduced following an upsurge of terrorist violence, but in fact applies generally and is not confined to alleged terrorist offences.[12] Article 3 of the Order follows the CLRC proposal to permit the tribunal of fact to draw inferences from the failure of the accused to mention facts at interview which he later relied upon in his defence. The Order however goes further than the CLRC proposals in permitting inferences to be drawn against the accused where he is found in specified incriminating circumstances and fails to account for these circumstances to the arresting constable (Article 5). Similarly, inferences may be drawn against the accused who is found in the vicinity of the scene of a crime and who fails to account for this to a constable who finds him there (Article 6). The Order also follows the recommendations of the CLRC in permitting inferences to be drawn from silence at trial (Article 4).

The arguments for reform

The arguments for modifying the right to silence along the lines recommended by the CLRC and the Home Office Working Group can be identified as follows.

i. It is natural to defend oneself against an allegation made by a person in authority. Failure to do so is therefore suggestive of guilt, in the absence of some explanation.

ii. A significant number of criminals avoid being charged or, if charged avoid conviction, by remaining silent at interview thereby depriving the police of the investigative opportunities presented by interview.

iii. A significant number of criminals escape conviction by not disclosing their defence to the police and then ambushing the court of trial by producing a new defence which the prosecution are then in no position to refute.

iv. It is a positive advantage to the police and the prosecution that any defence is raised in the course of interview. This prevents ambush defences and allows the police the opportunity to test the defence raised in the course of interview and to carry out further investigations to confirm or refute any defence raised.

---

[12] Jackson (1990).

v.   Modifying the right to silence as proposed would carry no substantial risks for the innocent suspect, who is adequately protected by other safeguards, notably access to legal advice in the police station.[13]

vi. That suspects who presently exercise the right to silence would be more likely to answer police questions and disclose any defence they wished to raise, if cautioned that if they did not do so they would be less likely to be believed and that it might have a bad effect on their case if the failed to do so.

The research

The purpose of this study is to attempt to quantify the exercise of the right to silence and to test some of the assumptions underlying the arguments set out above.

Chapter 2 – seeks to identify the circumstance in which a suspect can be said to be rely upon the right to silence, and to calculate the incidence of reliance on silence in the research sample.

Chapter 3 – seeks to test the assumption that exercise of the right to silence is a factor in a significant number of cases which terminate after arrest without further action being taken.

Chapter 4 – seeks to determine whether exercise of the right to silence is a significant factor in acquittals and discontinued cases.

Chapter 5 – seeks to identify what is meant by "ambush defence" and seeks to determine the incidence of ambush defences in cases which go to trial.

Chapter 6 – examines the assumption that it is advantageous for any defence to be raised in the course of interview because it provides the police with the opportunity to test that defence in the course of interview and to conduct further investigations to refute or confirm the defence raised.

Chapter 7 – considers the implications of the research for the current debate about reforming the right to silence.

---

[13] This argument is not addressed directly in this report, but see Sanders (1988).

The research sample

The study is based on a sample of 1080 cases, collected between 1986 and 1988.[14] The cases were collected consecutively from six police stations, with two drawn from each of three police forces. The research method was to track each case from point of arrest or report until final disposal. All evidence on the case file was noted, and the file was monitored at every stage of the proceedings. As far as possible interviews were conducted with every police officer or prosecutor who made a decision in relation to the case or had a significant input. The research was conducted on the basis that suspects, police officers, prosecutors and the police stations and forces involved would remain anonymous. Cases are identified by five or six-character codes, thus the code AHJ46 indicates the 46th juvenile suspect from police station H in force A.

---

[14] The research project was funded by the Economic and Social Research Council and was primarily concerned with the discretion to charge and to prosecute. The research team was Roger Leng, Mike McConville, Andrew Sanders, Vanessa Saxton and Robert Wight. The major findings of the research have been published in McConville *et al* (1991).

2. EXERCISE OF THE RIGHT TO SILENCE

Identifying significant exercise of the right to silence

A person being interviewed by the police has a right not to answer any question and a right not to disclose any particular fact in his answers if he so wishes. In one sense, anybody who declines to answer a question or who fails to disclose a relevant fact may be said to exercise the right to silence. However, if the purpose of calculating the numbers of suspects exercising the right is to inform the debate about whether the law should be modified, it would be misleading to include all those who are silent at some stage of the interview.

There are three reasons for this.

i. The present debate focuses on the effects of silence on the progress of the case beyond the interview stage

In many cases a failure or refusal to answer a specific question or disclose a particular fact will be temporary. As many studies have indicated one of the objectives of police interrogation is to overcome reluctance to speak.[1] The structure of the law surrounding police detention implicitly permits the police to hold a silent suspect in the hope of overcoming his silence. Where a suspect is initially silent but later answers all questions, any problem related to silence is overcome and the case cannot support an argument for law reform. Thus, in such cases the suspect has exercised his right to silence, but not in a way which is significant for the current debate. Similarly a suspect who refuses to respond to questions to which he has already provided an answer cannot be said to be exercising the right in a way which is significant for the purposes of the current debate.

In order to determine whether there has been a significant exercise of the right to silence it is necessary to consider the records of all custodial interviews and other informal interchanges between the suspect and the police. The right should be considered to be exercised only where the suspect is successful in maintaining silence on a particular matter.

---

[1] Irving and Hilgendorf (1980), Irving (1980), Moston *et al* (1992A).

ii. A suspect may answer questions but not disclose a defence

A suspect exercises the right to silence when, having been asked a relevant question, and having been given a reasonable opportunity to do so, he fails to disclose a particular matter which he later raises or intends to raise in his defence. Thus, a suspect who apparently answers all questions may be exercising the right to silence. Where no charges follow or the case does not reach court it will be normally impossible to determine whether the suspect did not disclose his proposed defence. Where a case reaches court, whether the suspect was silent in this sense can be determined by comparing the record of the trial with the record of interview. In a few cases which are disposed of without trial it may be possible to detect non-disclosure of a defence at interview, where the proposed defence is indicated in the course of correspondence between the defence and the CPS or in the course of plea bargaining.

This reasoning applies only where the suspect fails to disclose some factual matter on which he intends to rely in his defence. Thus, it could not be said that the defendant has failed to disclose his defence, where the defence raised in court rests on the proper legal significance of admitted facts (eg whether a particular knife is 'offensive *per se*'), or involves simply disputing whether the prosecution case proves the offence beyond reasonable doubt.[2]

Thus, a calculation of the extent to which the right to silence is exercised should include cases in which the suspect answers questions but fails to disclose a relevant defence which is later raised in court or indicated in pre-trial negotiations.

iii. Silence is significant only where it relates to the suspect's own involvement

In order to determine what is a significant exercise of the right to silence it is necessary to consider the scope of proposals to change the present law. In order to assess arguments for reform, it is necessary to estimate the proportion of cases on which the proposed reform would have an impact. Thus, any cases in which the suspect is silent on some matter, but which would not be affected by the proposed reform, should not be considered as a significant exercise of the right to silence for present purposes.

The suspect who refuses to name his accomplices or provide evidence against them clearly relies upon his right to be silent in the face of police questions. However, an examination of existing authoritative

---

[2] These issues are explored more fully in Chapter 5.

reform proposals indicates that this category would not be covered (except perhaps indirectly) by any of the proposed modifications to the right to silence. Thus, under the proposals of the CLRC, a jury would be entitled to draw such inferences as appear proper *against the accused* where he had failed to mention a fact during interrogation which he later relied upon at trial. It would also be possible to treat the earlier failure to mention the defence as corroboration of the evidence *against the accused*. Consistent with these reforms the CLRC recommended a revised form of caution which would warn the suspect of the possibility of inferences being drawn *against him*. The Home Office Working Group in substance adopted these proposals.

Similarly under the Criminal Evidence (Northern Ireland) Order Article 3, inferences may be drawn *against the accused* where he failed to mention any fact which he later relied upon at trial. Further, Articles 5 and 6 permit specific inferences to be drawn *against an accused* who fails to account for some incriminating mark or possession of an incriminating object, or for his presence near the scene of a crime. These provisions are coupled with a new caution, by which the suspect is warned that inferences may be drawn *against him* and that his silence may be treated as corroborating evidence.

The proposals of the CLRC and the Home Office Working Group and the reform embodied in the Northern Ireland Order, present three models for modification of the right to silence. In each case the suspect may suffer adverse consequences through his failure either to incriminate himself or to offer a defence. No adverse consequence would follow from failure to give evidence concerning a possible accomplice. Equally, the caution required under each model is designed to pressure the suspect to answer questions concerning his own culpability but does not appear to be designed or calculated to persuade a suspect to give evidence against others. It thus appears that present concern about the effects of silence do not include the extent to which silence during interview deprives the police of potential evidence against persons other than the person being interviewed.[3] Thus, it is argued that calculations of the extent of silence for

---

[3] One of the objectives of police interrogation is to obtain information about persons other than the immediate suspect. Indeed in a number of cases in the present study, the primary or only objective of interrogation was to obtain evidence against another person. However it appears that the police respect the suspect's desire to withhold details of an accomplice's involvement, provided that the suspect himself confesses. For instance in CCJ33 a sixteen year old boy admitted shoplifting but refused to name another boy who had been with him. The police made no apparent further attempt to discover the identity of the accomplice. See also Dixon (1990), pp. 40–41.

the purpose of the current debate should exclude cases in which the suspect's silence relates only to other persons.

It should also be pointed out that in terms of the law of evidence the failure of a suspect to incriminate himself is of more significance than the failure of a suspect to incriminate others. The reason for this is that whereas a confession is admissible against its maker, such out of court statements are never admissible against another person, and even where such evidence is tendered in direct testimony in court it is traditionally treated as being dubious if emanating from a possible accomplice.[4]

Thus, for the purposes of calculating the extent of the exercise of the right to silence, cases in which the suspect answers questions relating to his own involvement but refuses to answer questions relating to the involvement of others, should be excluded.

A review of estimates of the extent of silence

A number of researchers over the past twenty five years have attempted to calculate the extent of exercise of the right to silence in police interview. These studies are difficult to compare because of variations in the manner of collecting the case samples. A common factor is that the researchers do not identify their criteria for determining when the right to silence is exercised. This suggests that the identification of cases in which the right to silence is exercised has been considered to be unproblematic. It seems likely therefore that most estimates simply relate to cases in which the suspect was silent in relation to some or all questions.

Zander's study 1979

Zander examined the case papers for a sample of 282 cases tried at the Old Bailey. He found that 12 defendants (4 per cent) had relied upon the right to silence. Of these 9 were convicted.

Mitchell's study 1983

Mitchell examined the case papers for a sample of 400 cases tried at Worcester Crown Court. Of 394 defendants who had been formally questioned by the police, 17 (4.3 per cent) exercised the right of silence. The number of these defendants who were convicted is not recorded.

Baldwin & McConville's study 1980

Baldwin and McConville examined the case papers for 1000 cases heard in the Birmingham Crown Court and 476 cases drawn from various Crown Court centres in London. The Birmingham sample included 500 guilty

---

[4] Tapper (1990) 229–237.

pleas and 500 not guilty pleas. The figures for the London sample were 205 guilty pleas and 271 not guilty pleas. The researchers found that no statement was made by the accused in 3.8 per cent of the Birmingham sample and 6.5 per cent of the London sample. These figures do not purport to represent the extent of silence in the two samples, since they include cases where no interview took place and exclude cases in which the defendant was silent in relation to some questions only.

McKenzie and Irving's study 1988

McKenzie and Irving observed two samples of 68 interviews with suspects in the same police station in two successive years, 1986 and 1987. In 1986 a total of 8 suspects (11 per cent) did not answer some or all questions of substance. In 1987, 11 suspects (15 per cent) did not answer some or all questions of substance. In a further sample of 100 files relating to concluded cases, a total of 16 per cent of suspects did not answer some or all questions of substance. The outcomes of cases in this study were not recorded.

Willis' study 1988

The study conducted by Willis *et al* for the Home Office, which was primarily deigned to assess the impact of tape recording on interviews with suspects, provides some data on the proportion of interviews in which no evidence was forthcoming. The figures given indicate that in the three areas in which the study was conducted no evidence resulted from the interview in 4 per cent, 3 per cent and 2 per cent of cases. These figures are not presented as estimates of the exercise of the right to silence although it seems likely that in most cases the explanation for no evidence being collected was silence. Data collection was by police officers involved in interviewing who filled in 'monitoring forms'. The problems associated with this are discussed below in relation to the studies conducted for the Home Office Working Group.

Sanders' study 1989

The study by Sanders *et al* analysed about 500 cases in which an interrogation took place. The methodology was to attend interviews or to analyse tapes or transcripts, where attendance was not possible. 2.8 per cent of suspects were silent; 5.3 per cent made flat denials without explanation; 38 per cent made denials with some explanation; 54 per cent made some sort of admission.

The methods of analysis chosen do not permit an accurate calculation of exercise of the right to silence. In particular it is not known how many of the 'flat denial' category had failed to disclose a line of defence which was raised later in court. Also it is not known to what extent those suspects who made explained denials or who made admissions, also refused to answer some questions. This study did not record outcomes.

The Metropolitan Police Study for the Home Office Working Group[5]

This study was conducted in 10 Metropolitan Police divisions in 1987. The records of 1,558 interviews were examined, some suspects being interviewed more than once. The criteria for selecting the case sample are not stated. It was found that in 6 per cent of the cases the suspect refused to answer any questions from the start of the interview, and that in a further 6 per cent the suspect failed to answer any questions relevant to the offence. In 11 per cent of the cases the suspect failed to answer some questions relevant to the offence. The study concludes that 23 per cent of interviewees exercised their right of silence in one form or another.

This study does not record how many silent suspects were ultimately convicted, however it does indicate that more than 40 per cent of suspects who were silent at some stage, were not charged.

The West Yorkshire Police study for the Home Office Working Group[6]

A study similar to that carried out by the Metropolitan police was carried out by the West Yorkshire Police in 1988. The records of 3,095 interviews were examined, some suspects being interviewed more than once. The criteria for selecting the case sample are not stated. It was found that in 2.3 per cent of cases the suspect refused to answer any questions from the start of the interview, and that in a further 2.8 per cent the suspect failed to answer any questions relevant to the offence. In 7.3 per cent of cases the suspect failed to answer some questions relevant to the offence. The study concludes that 12.3 per cent of interviewees exercised their right of silence in one form or another.

This study does not record how many silent suspects were ultimately convicted, however it does indicate that 63 per cent of suspects who were totally silent and about 75 per cent of suspects who refused to answer some or all relevant questions, were not charged.

---

[5] Home Office (1989) Appendix C.
[6] Home Office (1989) Appendix C.

The two police studies and also Willis' study (discussed above) may fail to give an accurate estimate of the extent of exercise of the right to silence for the following reasons.

i.   The studies were not designed to identify cases in which the suspect answered questions but failed to disclose a line of defence which was later raised in court.

ii. The studies did not assess the number of cases in which the suspect was still maintaining the right to silence at the end of the interview.

iii. The studies give a misleading impression of the number of suspects who relied upon silence because the sample consists of individual interviews rather than all interviews conducted with the suspect during a single period of detention.[7] Thus, an individual suspect may figure in the sample as many times as he or she has been interviewed.[8] This is likely to distort the findings since some suspects who are silent at first interview are likely to be re-interviewed.

iv. These studies depended upon data collection by police officers. There are dangers of inconsistency where data collection is the responsibility of many different hands. There is also a risk of partiality. Organisations representing all grades in the police service have campaigned for many years to change the law relating to the right to silence.[9] Officers may believe that the campaign is more likely to be successful if a high incidence of reliance on the right is recorded, and it is possible that this may have influenced data collection.

Moston, Stephenson and Williamson's study 1992

The researchers collected data by means of questionnaires filled in by the interviewing officers, relating to 1067 "CID" cases in which interviews were held. They found that 8 per cent of suspects refused to answer all questions and a further 8 per cent refused to answer some questions, suggesting that a total of 16 per cent of suspects (174 cases) relied upon

---

[7] This criticism has been noted by Superintendent Tom Williamson who was responsible for the Metropolitan Police Study, Moston *et al* (1992B).

[8] In Brown's 1989 study 19 per cent of all suspects were interviewed more than once, including 6 per cent who were interviewed three or more times: Brown (1989), p. 44, Table 5.1.

[9] See for instance memoranda of evidence submitted to the Royal Commission on Criminal Procedure by the Association of Chief Police Officers and the Police Superintendents Association.

silence to some extent. The number of cases in which silent suspects were convicted is not recorded.

These findings are difficult to interpret. It is clear that they include cases in which the suspect eventually admitted the offence, as well as cases in which the suspect raised a defence or denied the charge. Thus, of the 174 'silence' cases, 33 (19%) made some form of confession or admission, whereas 50 'silent' suspects denied the allegation against them. It should also be noted that no attempt was made to identify cases in which the suspect maintained silence to the end of the interview. It is also not clear that the questionnaire was designed in order to clearly identify silence cases. The officers completing the questionnaire were instructed that the right to silence could be said to be used when a suspect declined to answer a question, either through evasion, silence or by saying 'No comment'. The difficulty with this instruction is that it might lead an officer to include within the silence category, what he or she considers to be evasive lies.

The study is also subject to the same criticisms as the studies commissioned by the Home Office Working Group, relating to inconsistencies of data collection and potential partiality of the collectors.

McConville and Hodgson's study 1992

This research was primarily concerned with the provision of legal advice in police stations. The researchers attended police interviews in 159 cases, between October 1991 and April 1992. In 2.5 per cent of cases the suspect answered no questions, whereas in 27 per cent, the suspect was selectively silent. Although, the total proportion of suspects who were silent at some stage of the interview is 29.5 per cent, the researchers argue that this figure is not a proper representation of the extent of exercise of the right to silence. The total figure is an over representation because it includes cases in which silence was temporary only, as well as cases in which the silence involved a failure to respond to irrelevant questions or questions which did not relate to the suspect's own involvement. It is also probable that the sample over-represents the extent of silence in cases in general, because a legal adviser was present at every interview. A number of studies have demonstrated a strong correlation between silence and the presence of a legal adviser at interview.[10]

Baldwin's study 1992

This research was based on 400 video recordings and 200 audio recordings of police interviews with suspects, collected from 6 police

---

[10] Moston *et al* (1992B), Baldwin (1992).

stations, 4 from the West Midlands Force, 1 from the West Mercia Force and 1 from the Metropolitan Force, in 1989 and 1990. The sample was not claimed to be representative because officers had a discretion whether or not to video-tape interviews, in particular it seems likely that the video-taped sample contained an over representation of more serious cases. There was a complete refusal to answer questions in 1.7 per cent of cases. In a further 18 per cent, the suspect declined to answer some questions. Although Baldwin does not seek to identify precisely the cases in which the suspect could be said to rely on the right to silence, he notes that in many cases the silence was temporary, related to an irrelevant question, or was related to the involvement of another person. For interviews attended by a legal representative the rate of silence was higher: 2.8 per cent of suspects were completely silent and a further 31 per cent declined to answer some questions.

The exercise of the right to silence in the present study

The extent of reliance on the right to silence during police interview in the present study was calculated by identifying cases in which:

i.   the suspect refused to answer all substantial questions;

ii. the suspect answered some questions but persisted in refusing to answer some substantial questions relating to his or her own involvement;

iii. the suspect denied the offence and did not disclose any ground of defence, having been given a reasonable opportunity to do so, where such a defence was later raised in court or indicated in pre-trial negotiations;

iv. the suspect denied the offence but failed or refused to give an explanation for a particular incriminating fact, where he was clearly invited to give such an explanation.

In relation to category iii., the suspect is considered to have exercised the right to silence only where the defence raised in court depended upon either, evidence which the defendant had a reasonable opportunity to mention to the police, or on some positive assertion (eg that the defendant had been under duress) which had not previously been made by the defendant. A case is not included in category iii. where the defence in court is based on simple denial, consistent with denial at interview, coupled with testing the prosecution case.

In relation to category iv., the term 'particular incriminating fact' means: either, a situation in which the accused was found in possession of an incriminating object (eg firearm or suspected stolen goods); or, was

15

found with an incriminating substance (e.g. blood) or mark (e.g. a bruise or rip) on his person or clothing; or, a situation in which the accused was found near the scene of a suspected crime. For the purposes of the present study the suspect is treated as exercising the right to silence where he fails to give an account of such incriminating fact because in these circumstances an evidential inference might be drawn against the accused at trial under Articles 5 or 6 Criminal Evidence (Northern Ireland) Order 1988.[11] It may be noted that although such cases would be covered by the Northern Irish legislation it is questionable whether cases in this category would necessarily involve exercise of the right to silence. For instance a suspect who vigorously denied knowledge of an incriminating mark on his clothing should not be considered as exercising the right to silence, but would be covered by Article 5 on the basis that he failed to account for the presence of the mark. In fact, this issue of categorization did not prove to be a problem in the present study since all cases in which the suspect failed to account for a particular fact involved a refusal to answer some or all questions.

For the purpose of calculating the extent of reliance on the right to silence it is considered that the right is not exercised in the following circumstances:

i. where the suspect initially refused to answer some questions but answered all substantial questions before the termination of the interview or interviews;

ii. where the suspect refused to answer questions substantially the same as earlier questions which he had already answered;

iii. where the suspect answered questions relating to his own involvement but refused to answer questions relating to the involvement of others.

---

[11] Under Art 5 Criminal Evidence (Northern Ireland) Order 1988, a failure by an arrested person to account for an incriminating object, substance or mark, may be treated as evidence against that person at any subsequent committal proceedings or trial. The object, substance or mark must be in the arrested person's possession, on his person, clothing or footwear, or in the same place in which he is arrested. The object, substance or mark will be incriminating if the constable reasonably concludes that its presence is attributable to the commission of a crime by the arrested person. Evidential inferences may be drawn only where the constable has informed the arrested person of his or her suspicions and asked the arrested person to account for the incriminating object, substance or mark. Under Art 6 evidential inferences may be drawn against a person who was arrested near to the scene of a suspected crime and at about the same time, and who declined to account for his presence there. An inference may be drawn only if a constable reasonably believed that the presence of the suspect was attributable to the commission of the offence, and had informed the arrested person of this and requested him to account for his presence.

The findings

Of 848 cases in which interviews took place, the right to silence was exercised in 38 cases (4.5 per cent). There were also 11 cases in which the suspect refused to answer some questions but which as argued above should not be treated as cases in which there was a significant exercise of the right to silence. These amount to 1.3 per cent of cases in which interviews were held. Thus of a total of 49 cases in which there was some silence in interview, in 38 cases (78 per cent of the silence cases) the right to silence was relied upon, whereas in 11 cases (22 per cent of the total silence sample), the suspect was silent but ultimately did not exercise the right to silence.

These figures suggest that other research studies which count exercise of the right to silence in terms of those suspects who refuse to answer some questions, will over-state the exercise of the right. The true incidence of the right to silence in interview is likely to be about three quarters of the number of suspects who are silent in relation to some or all questions.

Table 2.1 **Incidence of the right to silence**

	Total interviewed	Exercise of RTS	Silence not RTS
Adults	517	27 (5%)	9 (1.7%)
Juveniles	331	11 (3.3%)	2 (0.6%)
TOTALS	848	38 (4.5%)	11 (1.3%)

Silence and repeat interviews

It is assumed by the police that a suspect may be held for further interview if the first interview is not productive. It is apparent from Table 2.1 that about one quarter of suspects who were initially silent did not ultimately persist in exercising the right to silence. The data was analysed to determine the extent to which the police used repeat interviews as a means of combatting silence.

In the present study two or more interviews were held in 101 cases amounting to 12 per cent of all the cases in which interviews took place. Among the 49 cases in which the suspect was silent at some stage during interview, second or subsequent interviews were held in 6 cases (12 per cent).

Of the 38 cases in which the right to silence was exercised there were subsequent interviews in 2 cases. The general lack of subsequent interviews in these cases may suggest that the police did not attach much importance to obtaining a confession in these cases or did not anticipate success.

Of the 6 cases in which the suspect was silent at some stage of the interview(s) but ultimately answered all substantial questions relating to his own involvement, subsequent interviews were held in 3 cases (2 interviews in 2 cases, 3 interviews in 1). In each of these three cases there was some evidence that the successful interview had been preceded by an unrecorded discussion between the interviewer and the suspect.[12] Thus, in BKA104, the suspect answered 'No reply' to all questions at first interview, but immediately confessed to the offence at his second interview one hour and twenty minutes later. Similarly, in ATA116, the suspect made no reply to all questions in his first interview, but answered questions co-operatively from the outset in his second interview, six hours later. In both cases the immediate readiness of the suspect to answer questions in the second interview, without preliminaries may suggest that this followed some other discussion. In CEA110, the interviewing officer opened the third interview by referring to an earlier discussion in these terms: 'You have intimated that you wish to tell me about the matters which I have spoken to you about earlier'.

Legal advice

In the research sample as a whole, solicitors or their representatives attended some or all interviews in 80 (10 per cent) of the 825 interrogation cases for which this information was available. In relation to the 38 suspects who exercised the right to silence, 9 (24 per cent) had a solicitor for some or all interviews, and a further 7 (18 per cent) received legal advice in person or by telephone prior to interview. These findings support other research which has demonstrated a correlation between silence and the presence of a legal adviser.[13] The issue of the nature of the relationship between silence and legal advice is most fully discussed in McConville and Hodgson (1992).

Outcomes

Of the 34 cases in which the right to silence was exercised and the outcome known, the largest group of 16 cases (47 per cent) ended in convictions, 3 cases (9 per cent) ended with not guilty verdicts, in 6 cases

---

[12] Maguire (1988) found that police custody officers did not permit other officers to bend the rules by having informal discussions with suspects. However Irving and McKenzie (1989) found that whereas in most cases custody officers refused unofficial access to suspects, this did occur in some cases.
[13] Moston et al (1992B), Baldwin (1992).

(18 per cent) proceedings were started but later dropped and no further action was taken in 9 cases (26 per cent).

In relation to the 11 cases in which the suspect was silent at some stage of the interview but did not persist in exercise of the right to silence, convictions were obtained in 7 (63 per cent).

Table 2.2 Outcomes in cases in which the suspect was silent at some stage in interview

Outcome	Exercise of RTS	Silent not RTS	Total
Guilty plea	9	7	16
Guilty verdict after trial	7	0	7
Not guilty	3	1	3
Dropped *	6**	2	8
No further action	9	1	10
Not known	4	-	4
Total	38	11	49

* Note that the 'Dropped' category includes withdrawn cases, discontinued cases and cases in which a not guilty verdict follows the offering of no evidence by the prosecution.

** The figure of 6 for dropped cases in which the right to silence was exercised includes one case in which the defendant was bound over following a not guilty verdict when the prosecution offered no evidence.

Motives for silence

An important argument for modifying the right to silence is that the only significantly occurring motive for silence is guilt. Other motives have been suggested, in particular that answering questions or disclosing a defence to the allegation might disclose some fact embarrassing to the suspect.[14] However, these have been dismissed as fanciful[15] and it has been argued that if there really was a reasonable excuse for not disclosing a defence to the police, this can be put to the jury and they can consider it in deciding what inferences, if any, can be drawn from the accused's silence.

Although the present research cannot generally discern motives for silence, it is apparent that some suspects refuse to answer questions in

---

[14] Criminal Law Revision Committee (1972) para 35.
[15] Cross (1973), Williams (1987).

order to avoid incriminating others. This apparently occurred in five cases in which the suspect admitted his own role in the offence but refused to answer questions relating to others.

In view of the clear finding that the protection of others may be the motive for partial silence, it is possible that this may also be the operative motive in some cases where the suspect is either completely silent or refuses to answer some questions relating to his own role. This appeared to be the case in AHA54. The suspect was found with two other men in possession of a van containing stolen goods. After offering two implausible and conflicting excuses, A54 then refused to answer further questions. In fact he was later released after another man accepted responsibility for the stolen goods and the police were satisfied that A54 had nothing to do with the offence.

Arguments for modifying the right to silence rest upon an assumption that in all but exceptional cases, the only plausible motive for silence is guilt. In the present study it appeared that in 6 (12%) of the 49 cases in which the suspect was silent at some stages of the interview, the motive was to protect others. The actual proportion of cases in which the motive for silence was the protection of others may well be higher than this since in the majority of silence cases there is no means of determining the suspect's motives.

Thus, if arguments for reform rest upon an assumption that guilt is the only plausible motive for silence, those arguments will be weakened by the evidence presented here that the protection of others is the motive for silence in a small but significant proportion of silence cases.

Summary

For the purpose of the current debate about whether the law should be reformed, a suspect should be considered to exercise the right to silence only where he persists in refusing to answer some or all substantial questions relating to his own culpability, or where he fails to disclose a defence which he later relies upon at trial and which he might reasonably have been expected to mention in the circumstances.

Suspects relied upon the right to silence in 4.5 per cent of cases in which interviews were held. In a further 1.3 per cent of cases, the suspect was silent at some stage of the interview but did not ultimately rely upon the right to silence.

Suspects who exercised the right to silence were significantly more likely than other suspects to have had a solicitor present for some or all interviews. About half of all suspects exercising the right to silence were convicted.

Although it is often assumed that guilt is the only significantly occurring motive for silence, the present findings suggest that protecting others is a motive in a small but significant proportion of silence cases.

3. No Further Action Cases

A substantial number of arrests end in a decision to take no further action against the arrested person. Where this decision is taken by the custody officer at the point when the suspect is released from detention it may be described as a "refused charge" decision. In other cases, the suspect may be granted bail to return to the police station and may be told of the decision to take no proceedings on his or her return, or more commonly will be told of the decision to take no proceedings by telephone call which has the effect of releasing the suspect from bail. The decision to take no further action includes two categories of case which in formal terms do not signal an investigative failure. These are "Detected, no proceedings", an outcome which is appropriate where it is impossible or undesirable to proceed against the suspect, for instance because of his or her health, and "No crime", an outcome which reflects a judgment by the police that the reported incident never took place or did not amount to a criminal offence. Apart from these two categories, the decision to take no further action may be taken to indicate an unsatisfactory outcome and an investigative failure.

A bundle of assumptions relating to no further action decisions underpin the arguments for modifying the right to silence. These assumptions are:

i.   that a decision to take no further action is indicative of a failure of the investigation;

ii. that a significant number of such decisions are linked to the exercise of the right to silence;

iii. that if suspects could be induced to answer police questions rather than remain silent, investigations which are currently aborted might lead to prosecutions.

The purpose of this Chapter is to examine these three assumptions: by giving an account of no further action decisions in the research sample; by identifying cases in which NFA decisions are linked to the silence of the suspect; and by considering whether there is a significant advantage in terms of the strength of the prosecution case, where the suspect answers questions rather than remains silent.

The case sample

For the purposes of the present study a case is classified as NFA where no proceedings or caution follow in relation to the conduct for which the suspect was arrested or reported. Thus, a case is classified as NFA where, for instance, a person is arrested for suspected theft of a motor vehicle, but proceeded against only for road traffic offences which come to light in the course of the investigation. However, a case is not treated as NFA where the police choose to proceed on a lesser or different charge relating to the conduct for which he was arrested.

An account of no further action decisions

The research sample contained 279 cases which terminated with no further action. In 268 cases there was a formal decision to take no further action. Eleven cases fizzled out without any formal decision being recorded. These eleven cases which included 2 in which the right to silence was exercised are not considered further in this Chapter.

Of the 268 cases in which a formal NFA decision was made: in 9 cases the decision to take no further action followed the exercise of the right to silence by the suspect (this group will be analysed separately below); in 114 cases the police were satisfied that the suspect was not guilty of the offence for which he had been arrested or reported; in 94 cases the suspect denied the offence but the police were not convinced of his innocence; in 24 cases the NFA decision was taken on policy grounds; in 25 cases the NFA decision followed the withdrawal of the complaint by the victim; and in 2 cases the reason for the NFA decision was not discovered.

Table 3.1 Analysis of NFA decisions

	No.	%of all NFAs
Right to silence	9	4%
Police satisfied of innocence	114	43%
Denial. Police not satisfied	94	35%
Policy grounds	24	9%
Complaint withdrawn	25	9%
Not known	2	1%
TOTAL	268	101%

Innocent suspects

In 114 cases, amounting to 42 per cent of all NFAs, the police were apparently satisfied that the suspect was not guilty of the offence for which he was arrested. In many cases no further action was the natural and expected result of police arrest policies. For instance, where the police operate a policy of arresting drivers who cannot account for their possession of a vehicle, release without action follows immediately that ownership or authority to drive is established. The sample contained 17 such cases. Release without action is also the expected result where person are arrested as part of a 'trawl' of persons known to have records for particular types of offences or where the police operate a blanket policy to arrest all persons within a particular class (eg all occupants of a house in which drugs have been found).

A further category in which release without action was the inevitable result involved eight cases in which the person arrested was never considered to be a criminal suspect by the police and was apparently arrested and interviewed primarily as a witness.[1]

NFA on policy grounds

In 24 cases the police had sufficient evidence to charge or to caution but decided to take no further action on policy grounds. In this context a 'policy ground' means any consideration apart from those relating to proof of an offence. The characterisation of a decision as being based on policy grounds was made by the researcher. In many cases the policy ground in question fell within the criteria for non-prosecution set out in the *Home Office Guidelines on Cautioning* and the *Code for Crown Prosecutors*. In other cases the decision to take no further action served some other policy goal of the police such as rewarding an informer or to avoid exposing mistakes or improper conduct by the police.

NFA after complaint withdrawn

In 25 cases no action was taken after the complaint was withdrawn or because the injured party would be unavailable to give evidence. The largest group of these cases involved minor violence. However, the police are also willing to take no action at the request of the injured party in other

---

[1] There is no lawful authority for arresting a witness. In each of these cases the reason for arrest was recorded as the offence to which the person in question was believed to be a witness. An example of this category of case is BKA80. A man was seen with a loaded gun in a pub in the company of BKA80. There was no suggestion of any offence by A80 and indeed the file summary by the arresting officer describes A80 as being 'invited to attend the police station so that enquiries could be made'. The custody record recounts that A80 was asked to sit in the front office of the police station and that he was told that he was free to leave if he wished. However when he decided to exercise this option one hour later at 00.30 am, A80 was formally arrested. He was eventually interviewed for 29 minutes at noon on the following day and then released.

cases such as theft which involve an invasion of an individual's personal interests.

NFA where the police are not convinced of the suspect's innocence

In 94 cases (35 per cent of all NFAs) a decision was made to take no further action on grounds of insufficient evidence where the police were not satisfied that the suspect was innocent. It should be noted however that these were not all cases in which the police believed the suspect to be guilty. In many cases there was a genuine reasonable doubt.

Cases of small perceived worth may be dropped in the face of a denial even where there is a reasonable prospect of a conviction. Thus, in CCA56/57 two men seen bending down near the liquor shelf in a store, then left the store and were seen to enter a bush. Two brandy bottles were found in the bush. The men were released after flatly denying stealing the brandy. The police may also accept a denial or exculpatory account at face value without further investigation. Thus, in BWA78 the suspect denied theft of building materials and offered to prove that they had been purchased legitimately. In view of his strenuous denials, he was released without being asked to prove ownership as he had offered to do.

It should not be assumed that the police are necessarily frustrated where no action is taken but suspicion remains. The police may be quite content with such an outcome where, for instance, the suspect provides valuable information against others, or where the police have sufficient evidence to proceed against other suspects whom they consider to be the prime movers. The police may also be unconcerned about taking no action where the suspect in question is already subject to pending proceedings for other offences.

Exercise of the Right to Silence in NFA cases

As discussed in Chapter 2, a suspect should be considered to be exercising the right to silence not only where he refuses to answer all or some questions in police interview, but also where he answers questions but fails to disclose a defence which is later raised in court, or which he intends to raise if the case goes to court. In relation to cases in which no further action is taken it is impossible to determine how many suspects fall into the second category. An indication that a suspect was withholding a defence would be that he answered questions but failed to account for a particular incriminating fact, such as possession of a prohibited substance or article, or presence at the scene of a crime. However, in the research sample, there were no NFA cases in which the suspect answered questions but failed to account for a particular incriminating fact.

The sample contained 9 cases which ended with a decision to take no further action in which the suspect declined to answer some or all questions. However, in only one case was the suspect totally silent in relation to an alleged offence. Thus, AHA67 gave a full exculpatory account of his actions at the scene of the alleged offence, ATJ21 said that he understood why he was being interviewed and then claimed to have forgotten relevant events before relying on silence, AHJ28, CEA64 and BWJ19 denied that they had committed any offence to the arresting officer, AHA54 gave two different accounts of the incriminating circumstances before deciding to say nothing further, both AHA01 and AHA22 admitted being at the race track where it was alleged the offence took place and AHA22 also denied the offence in interview.

NFA may be the result of factors other than silence

It should not be assumed that evidential weakness is the reason for all decisions to take no further action following exercise of the right to silence. In 4 of the 9 cases in which ended in NFA following exercise of the right to silence the operative reason did not relate to the strength of the evidence. Thus, in BWJ19, notwithstanding the suspect's total silence in interview, the police were advised by CPS that there was a provable case on the evidence which included identification by a store detective. The decision not to institute proceedings was taken only when it was realised that J19 had been sentenced at Crown Court for other offences between the commission of the present offence and the receipt of CPS advice. In ATJ21, the decision not to proceed against a thirteen year old boy was made on policy grounds after the police were satisfied that his school were dealing with the matter in an appropriate way. In AHA54 no proceedings were taken because the police were satisfied that A54 was not involved after another man admitted the offence.

The decision not to take no further action may also result from a combination of evidential weakness and other factors. Thus, in AHA67 it was alleged that A67 had attempted to rob an American tourist. In the course of arrest A67 had vehemently denied the charge and had claimed that the tourist had dropped his bag and that he had been trying to give the bag back to the tourist. In interview he refused to answer questions. The police decided not to charge because they anticipated that A67 would plead not guilty and that the tourist would not been available to give evidence. Although the suspect refused to answer all questions at the police station, he had offered a full justification for his actions on the street. Thus, the case is one in which the police were hampered by his refusal to admit the offence rather than by his refusal to offer an explanation for his actions. In view of the policy not to proceed unless the victim is available to give evidence, it seems that this case would have failed whatever response A67 had made at interview.

NFA for evidential weakness

In 5 silence cases evidential weakness was the primary reason for the decision to take no further action. However, in 3 of these cases the suspect's silence did not necessarily terminate the investigation and the NFA decision resulted from some other investigative failure.

In BWA27 the suspect was identified as the person who had seized a television which was on display outside a television shop and had escaped in a taxi. In interview he answered 'No answer' OR 'No reply' to all questions. He was bailed to return to the police station so that an identification parade could be held with the taxi driver. He answered bail but for reasons which were not clear no identity parade was ever held. His release without charge could be attributed to the failure to hold the identity parade rather than to his silence.

Failure of identification procedures was also a factor in the decision to take no further action in AHA01 and AHA22. Both cases were concerned with alleged greyhound race 'wrecking'. This practice involves obstructing a race in which the favourite looks likely to win, in order that the race should be declared void, thereby preventing substantial losses to the bookmakers. AHA22 refused to answer some questions and was released after the principal witness failed to pick him out at an identification parade. In the case of AHA01, the police arranged a confrontation between A01 and the principal witness at the racetrack. A01 was positively identified but was released without action because the identification procedure had been in breach of the relevant Home Office guidelines and the police accepted that the identification evidence would not be admissible in court.

Even where the investigation effectively terminates with the suspect's silence the police may not be particularly dissatisfied with the NFA decision. Thus, in AHJ28, the suspect, a known car thief was seen near a car which had recently been broken into. His clothes also fitted the description of clothes worn by the person who had broken into the car earlier and who had been seen running from the scene. In interview J28 said nothing. He was released without further action on the basis of lack of any direct evidence to associate him with the offence. Although the custody sergeant told researchers that it "broke my heart to have to let him go", it appeared that the investigating officer was not particularly dissatisfied with this outcome. As the officer explained, J28 was already being proceeded against for similar offences and it was not considered very important to add this offence to his list of charges. The degree of importance which the police attached to gaining sufficient evidence and charging in this case is reflected in the fact that J28 was held for 1 hour 50 minutes and was interviewed once.

Is the prosecution disadvantaged by silence?

Those who argue for the abolition or modification of the right to silence are primarily concerned that it assists the guilty to avoid prosecution and conviction. Although modification of the law as proposed by the CLRC and the Home Office Working Group would allow evidential inferences to be drawn against the silent suspect in certain circumstances, the primary aim of the proposed reform would be to induce those who might otherwise remain silent, to speak. Realistically, it must be accepted that the choice for the guilty suspect will be between silence and untrue denial, perhaps supported by an exculpatory explanation. Thus, the object of the proposed reform is to induce suspects to lie to the police rather than to say nothing. It appears to be assumed that it is advantageous for the police that the defendant should deny falsely rather than remain silent. In particular it is assumed that a denial provides opportunities for the exercise of interrogation techniques and further investigation, which are not available if the suspect remains silent. The actual nature of police responses to defences and denials is considered in Chapter 6. The purpose of this section is to test the hypothesis that denials offer greater investigative opportunities than silence.

This study is confined to two case samples: i. the 94 cases which ended with a decision to take no further action, in which the police were not satisfied of the suspect's innocence; ii. the 9 cases which ended in a decision to take no further action after the suspect exercised the right to silence.[2]

The reason for confining this study to these samples is as follows. The assumption is that the obstructive guilty suspect is better able to shield his guilt through silence rather than through lies, and that lies present the police with more investigative opportunities than are presented by silence. It is impossible to determine how many guilty suspects are successful in shielding their guilt. However, it is possible to identify the group of suspects who are i. not considered to be clearly innocent, and ii. successful in avoiding adverse consequences in terms of charge and conviction. If the research as a whole includes obstructive guilty suspects, some of them are likely to figure in the chosen samples.

---

[2] In one of these cases, AHA54, the police were satisfied that the suspect was innocent notwithstanding his silence.

The method adopted for this study was to analyse interviews to determine:

i. what sorts of answers were required in view of the questions asked;

ii. the nature of denials and defences raised by suspects.

NFA after answering questions

Of the 94 cases in which the suspect answered questions and was released without further action, in 57 cases the suspect was either required to account for some incriminating fact, or to give further information in support of his denial. In all of these cases the suspect provided the required account or information. In 35 cases, the nature of the allegation made by the police and the style of questioning meant that a simple denial was an adequate answer. Of the two remaining cases, in one there was no interview, in the other the information available was insufficient to permit analysis.

Allegation may be answered by simple denial

In many of the 35 cases in which the allegation put to the suspect could be answered by a simple denial, the evidence against the suspect was circumstantial only. Thus, in CCA68 the suspect was found in a telephone box soon after a hoax telephone call had been made. In ATJ30 and 31 two youths were found inside a derelict building but denied being there with intent to steal. In BKA110 a shed had been burnt down and A110 was suspected since he had been rebuffed as a suitor by the owner of the shed.

In a large group of cases the circumstantial evidence was simply that the suspect had had an opportunity to commit the offence. Thus in CEJ25, BKA10 and BKA33 the only basis for arrest was that the suspect lived at a house in which a crime had been committed. In 12 cases in which the suspect was released after denial, the only evidence linking the suspect to the offence came from an informant who had not given a formal statement, or from an alleged accomplice.

In one case only of this group were the police in a position to conduct further investigations to refute the suspect's denial. In CEA93 a man had sold a bicycle to a shop and gave A93's name. it was later discovered that the bicycle had been previously stolen. A93 completely denied that he had been the man who sold the bicycle. Had the police wished to pursue the case they could have arranged an identification procedure with the shopkeeper, although this was not in fact done.

In the cases discussed above, because of the nature of the evidence and the manner of questioning, a simple denial was a full and satisfactory answer to the allegation. In all but one of these cases the denial was inscrutable in the sense that apart from expressing disbelief, no further means of testing the veracity of the denial was available to the police. In these cases there were no facts asserted by the suspect which could be investigated; there were no accounts of movements or events which could be tested by cross-examination; there was no further evidence, apart from that implied in the initial allegation, which could be put to the suspect to cast doubt on his story.

Allegation requires suspect to account for incriminating fact or provide information

Analysis of the 57 cases in which the suspect accounted for an incriminating fact or provided evidence in his own defence, suggests that in 37, the suspect's story was effectively as inscrutable as a simple denial. Where the evidence available to the police is incomplete, the suspect is frequently able to present his defence in a way which disables further investigation. For instance 10 cases involved the classic 'man in the pub' defence. These were cases in which the suspect was found in possession of an incriminating article (typically stolen goods) and claimed that he had bought them from a man in the pub known only by a first name or of unknown identity. Further questioning would elicit a generalised description and claims of ignorance as to any other characteristic which might assist the police to identify the mystery man.

In other cases, once the suspect had given an excusory account of the relevant incriminating fact, there was no obvious further investigative ploy apart from to repeat the allegation or to suggest that the suspect was lying. This was typically the case where the relevant incriminating fact which the suspect was required to account for was merely circumstantial evidence. Thus, in CCJ08, a youth was seen running and wearing muddy clothing at 5 am in an area where a burglary had been committed. His explanation was that he was out for an early morning jog.

A straightforward excusory account may also effectively end the enquiry in cases where there is more positive evidence against the suspect. Thus, in ATJ08, a car alarm sounded and the suspect was seen running away. In interview he denied attempting to steal from the car and claimed that he had deliberately set the alarm off for fun. In ATJ20, a young boy who was found in possession of a stolen bicycle said that his brother had given it to him and that he had no idea that it was stolen. In CEA05, the suspect had approached an elderly man and offered to re-surface his drive. The elderly man reported this, stating that the suspect had demanded a grossly excessive sum for the job. The suspect was arrested for attempting to obtain money by deception. In interview he admitted offering to do the job but for a reasonable price. Similarly, in BKA49 a fire extinguisher salesman was arrested for attempting to obtain by deception after a shopkeeper reported that the salesman had claimed to be from the Fire Service. The salesman was released after denying ever making such a claim.

Inscrutability

Of 94 cases which ended in no further action but in which the police were not satisfied of the suspect's innocence, the story told by the suspect was inscrutable in 71 cases (75 per cent of the total). This suggests that in three quarters of the cases in this sample the police gained no advantage from the fact that the suspect chose to answer questions rather than to remain silent. There was a potential advantage for the police in the sense of some further investigative tactic indicated by the interview in 25 per cent of cases.

NFA after silence

As indicated above, in the majority of cases which end in NFA in which the suspect chooses to answer questions, this is of no apparent advantage to the investigation. However, this finding does not indicate whether the investigation was hampered in those cases in which the suspect relied upon the right to silence. Of the 9 NFA cases in which the suspect relied upon the right to silence at some stage of the interview, there appeared to be no particular disadvantage for the investigation in 6 cases.

> *AHA01* The suspect was arrested on suspicion of dog race 'wrecking' for the purpose of defrauding bookmakers. The police had relied upon an informant who had identified A01 but who was not willing to give a formal statement. In interview the suspect answered some questions, admitting that he had been at the race track on the relevant evening, but declined to answer specific allegations. In the absence of any admissible evidence, A01 was released without charge. Had the suspect flatly denied the charges put to him it is doubtful whether the police would have been in any better position to pursue the investigation since there was no specific incriminating evidence which the suspect was required to account for.

> *AHA22* (linked to AHA01 above) The evidence against A22 was that he had been seen stepping on to the track. His flat denial that he had done this amounted to a full answer to the evidence available and left little scope for further questions.

> *CEA64* A window had been smashed at night and a witness had thought that the perpetrator had run into a nearby park. A64

was found by police in the park but refused to answer any questions. The evidence against him was circumstantial only and if the suspect had denied any involvement the police would have had no particular basis on which to test his story.

BWJ19 The suspect was silent in the face of clear evidence from a reliable witness. Had he spoken it would have been difficult to deny the offence with any credibility. However, it is not clear that the prosecution case was prejudiced by his silence since a confession, admission or damaging statement by him would merely have bolstered an already strong and provable case.

AHA67 The suspect although silent in the police station had denied the alleged offence at the time of arrest. He claimed that he had not been tying to seize the victim's bag, but on the contrary had found the bag and had been trying to return it to its owner. On the evidence in the case this was rather implausible, and the suspect might have had difficulty sustaining the story under critical interview. However, like BWJ19, this was a case where the evidence was probably strong enough to sustain a conviction if the case had gone to court.

AHA54 The suspect resorted to silence only after raising two different unconvincing stories. Had he been charged, the prosecution would have gained an advantage because if he had tried to rely upon either of the excuses raised in interview or upon a new defence, evidence of inconsistency would have been admissible to disprove the defence raised in court.

In 3 cases there was a realistic prospect that the investigation might have benefitted from the suspect answering questions.

BWA27 A man had taken a television from a display outside a shop and escaped in a taxi. The taxi driver was later interviewed and picked out A27 as the thief. If A27 had been willing to participate in the interview, the police would have been in a position to put this direct evidence to him, this might have led to a successful conclusion to the case if the suspect had been persuaded that in view of the evidence his best course would be to admit the offence. If, however the suspect had simply denied the offence the police would have been left in the same position as if he had been silent. In both circumstances there would have ben good identification evidence but with no corroboration from the suspect himself. Interestingly, this case foundered after the police failed to arrange an identification parade which they had planned. The researchers were unable to discover the reason for this but the most likely explanations are that the witness refused to take part or that the police lost interest in the case after failing to obtain a confession.

AHJ28 The suspect was arrested close to the scene of the crime. There was therefore no question of him raising an alibi which might be tested. The only positive evidence against him was that his clothes were similar to those worn by a person thought to be the offender. As the case stood the evidence was not sufficient to warrant prosecution. If he had answered questions there might have been some scope for cross-examining him on any story raised.

ATJ21 The police had evidence from the victim which named J21. They were however doubtful about relying on the evidence of a child and even if they had wished to proceed they might have decided not to do so without some further evidence.

Whether or not the investigation is hampered where the suspect remains silent rather than answers questions, is ultimately unknowable. However, this analysis of the small group of silence cases which ended with no further action, suggests the following tentative conclusions. The stronger the evidence, the better the prospects for breaking down the suspect's defence if he chooses to speak. However, where the evidence is strong the benefit from persuading the suspect to speak may be insignificant because the evidence would be sufficient to sustain a conviction whether the suspect is silent or not.[3] Where the evidence is weak or merely circumstantial, the suspect may be able to answer the allegations with a simple denial or by a story which is inscrutable. Where this is the case, the benefit to the prosecution of inducing the suspect to speak rather than remain silent, will be minimal.

Summary

Arguments for reform of the right to silence are linked to concern about the large numbers of arrested suspects who are released without further action being taken against them. Analysis of these cases however indicates that this concern may be misdirected. In 62 per cent of NFA cases that outcome was satisfactory to the police, whereas in only 38 per cent was it considered that the investigation had failed. The right to silence was exercised in only 4 per cent of NFA cases. In 4 of the 9 cases which ended in NFA following exercise of the right to silence, it appeared that some factor other than evidential weakness was the major operative reason for the decision. Thus, there would be a potential advantage to the

---

[3] Similar findings are made in Moston *et al* (1992B).

prosecution in inducing the suspect to speak in only about 2 per cent of all NFA cases.

It is also assumed by proponents of reform that it would be advantageous to persuade silent suspects to answer questions. However, the study of NFA cases in which the suspect did answer questions suggests that in cases in which the police do not have sufficient independent evidence to charge, the suspect's answers are potentially useful to the investigation in only about 25 per cent of cases. The reason for this is that where the police conduct the interview on a weak evidential basis, it will often be possible for the suspect to answer the allegations put to him by a simple denial or a story which the police are not in a position to test or check. In these cases the suspect's denial or defence is inscrutable in the sense that apart from expressing disbelief, the police have no obvious means of testing the veracity of the accused's story.

It would be impossible to determine conclusively whether it would have benefitted the investigation if silent suspects had been induced to speak. However, analysis of the 9 NFA cases in which the suspect was silent casts some light on this issue. It was assumed that if a silent suspect were induced to speak he would deny the offence or raise a defence (findings discussed in Chapter 6 indicate that the police are successful in breaking down defences raised in interview in only 5.4 per cent of cases). In 6 cases it appeared that the suspect could have answered the allegations by an effectively inscrutable denial or defence.

These findings suggest that in the majority of cases in which suspects presently exercise the right to silence, there would be no clear advantage to the investigation in inducing the suspect to speak.

4. Acquittals

Cases in which a person is charged but no conviction obtained are treated as failures by the police and the Crown Prosecution Service. Such cases are seen as being wasteful of resources and high acquittal rates are seen as evidence that criminals have escaped their just desserts through procedural rules which are too favourable to the accused,[1] or through the gullibility of juries.[2] In particular it has been asserted that a substantial number of acquittals are linked to the exercise of the right to silence by the accused in both police interrogation and in the course of trial.[3]

The purpose of this Chapter is to provide an account of the acquittals in the research sample and to consider the extent to which these acquittals are linked to the exercise of the right to silence during police interrogation.

For present purposes an acquittal is treated as being any case in which a person has been formally charged but is not ultimately convicted or bound over for any offence relating to the incident for which that person was arrested or reported. Although in many cases binding over accompanies a formal acquittal (ie where the prosecution agree to drop charges in return for the defendant's agreement to be bound over), these cases are not treated as acquittals for the purposes of the present study. The reason for this is that by agreeing to be bound over, the accused accepts some degree of wrongdoing, and accordingly a bind over is viewed by the police and CPS as an appropriate and successful outcome in most cases.

The acquittal category as defined above includes cases which are discontinued under section 23(3) Prosecution of Offences Act 1985, cases which are withdrawn and cases in which no evidence is offered. It has been argued elsewhere that the particular mechanism adopted for dropping a case depends upon arbitrary factors and that neither the police nor the CPS attach significance to the manner in which a case is dropped.[4]

---

[1] Mark (1973).
[2] Gobert (1989).
[3] Lawton, (1987).
[4] McConville *et al* (1991), p. 152.

Accordingly, for the purposes of the present study, cases which are dropped prior to a contested trial are treated as a single category.

Of the 490 cases in which the suspect was charged 79 (16%) ended in acquittal as defined above. Of this group of cases 54 (11%) were dropped by the prosecution and in 25 (5%) acquittal followed a contested trial.

Dropped cases

Of the 54 dropped cases, 12 cases were dropped for policy reasons, 8 cases were dropped for reasons of technical difficulty, and 33 cases were dropped on grounds of insufficient evidence. In one case it was not possible to ascertain the reason why the case was dropped.

Policy reasons

The fact that a case is dropped does not necessarily indicate that the investigation has failed or has been obstructed. Where a case is dropped for policy reasons this is frequently seen as a satisfactory outcome. The sample included cases which were dropped on public interest grounds because the defendant was already facing similar charges or had been sentenced to a long term of imprisonment for other offences. Cases were also dropped for triviality, on health grounds and in order to secure the defendant as a prosecution witness.

Technical problems

This group includes cases in which it is either impossible or inappropriate to proceed because of some mistake or omission by the police or CPS, excessive delay or for reasons beyond the control of the prosecution.

Insufficient evidence

The 33 cases which were dropped for insufficient evidence included 5 in which the defendant had exercised the right to silence and 2 in which the defendant had initially refused to answer some questions but ultimately provided answers to all substantial questions. In neither of these two cases was the defendant's temporary silence linked to the dropping of the case. Thus, in BKA104 the defendant had denied a shoplifting allegation in his second interview. The case was dropped when it was realised that there was no evidence on the prosecution file to identify A104 as the man who had been seen stealing. In ATJ52, the defendant had been found in possession of a knife, he eventually answered all questions and denied having the knife for the purposes of causing injury. The case was dropped by CPS because there was no evidence that the knife was carried as an offensive weapon.

In the majority of these cases the evidential weakness was manifest from the outset, but the police had not sought advice prior to charging the defendant and the CPS proceeded with the case until it became apparent that the defendant would plead not guilty. Thus at the time when the data was collected, late discontinuances for evidential weakness and not guilty verdicts after no evidence was offered in court, appeared to be largely attributable to inadequate case vetting by the CPS.[5]

Cases dropped following exercise of the right to silence

In five cases charges were dropped where the suspect had asserted his right to silence during interrogation. Typically, these were cases in which the evidence was thin or non-existent, and in which the decision to charge had been motivated by a conviction that the suspect was guilty, confirmed as far as the police were concerned by the suspect's silence in interview.

> *AHJ38* the suspect was identified as a man who had broken into a car. He refused to answer any questions in interview. At court the prosecution offered no evidence after the defence intimated that they would challenge the prosecution evidence of identification.

> *BKA117* The defendant was arrested on the basis that he was a known associate of another man who was suspected of theft. In interview he refused to answer all questions. He was charged but the case was dropped after the accused elected jury trial. The ground for dropping the case was that it would not be economic to take such a trivial case to Crown Court in view of the possibility of an acquittal. In fact, short of the possibility of A117 pleading guilty, there was no prospect of conviction since the prosecution file contained no evidence whatsoever against him.

There was slightly more evidence in CCA118.

> *CCA118* The defendant had been with another man in a shop when the other man stole a suit. In interview he stated that he did not want to answer questions for fear of contradicting himself and that he would tell his story to one person only and that was his solicitor. A118 was charged as an accomplice to theft but was acquitted after the CPS offered no evidence at trial.

In two of the silence cases there was apparently sufficient evidence to charge but the evidential weakness emerged at a late stage of the case.

---

[5] McConville *et al* (1991), Chap 7.

BKA67 The defendant had been named as a person seen driving a car which had been taken without authority, and had been seen by the police in the vicinity of the same car soon after it had been dumped. The case was dropped after the main prosecution witness appeared very uncertain about his identification at committal proceedings.

BKA100 A middle aged man was charged with unlawful sexual intercourse and indecent assault in relation to two very young girls. In interview he admitted inviting the girls into his house and kissing them but then answered no further questions on the advice of his solicitor who was present. The evidence of the girls was thought to be corroborated by the evidence of the police surgeon who examined the girls. However, the police surgeon reversed his professional opinion having considered the medical evidence produced by the defence.

Acquittals after trial

Of the 25 acquittals following a contested trial, in 17 cases (68 per cent) the particular defence which had been raised in interview was raised successfully in court (this group included two cases in which the court held that there was no case to answer), in 6 cases a defence was raised in court which had not been raised at interview and 2 cases were dismissed for excessive delay.[6]

Defence raised in interview is successful in court

One of the assumptions underlying arguments to modify the right to silence is that it is advantageous to the police that the suspect should produce a defence or denial in interview rather than remain silent. The advantage is said to lie in the opportunity to test and undermine or disprove the defence raised. This assumption is contradicted (but not disproved) by the finding that the commonest explanation for acquittal after a contested trial is that the court accepted the defence initially raised in police interview.

Examination of the small group of acquittals following trial suggests that it is only in those cases where the police are in possession of strong independent evidence prior to the interview that they are in a strong position to undermine any defence raised by the accused. Where there is a lack of independent evidence against the accused there is

---

[6] These were technically cases in which a procedural defence was raised for the first time at court. However, in both cases the defence lawyer had indicated that if the case had proceeded the accused would have raised the same defence which he had indicated in the police interview.

frequently little the police can do to disprove or undermine the defence raised.

An example of a case in which the police had no basis to undermine the accused's defence was CCA10. The defendant was charged with possessing an offensive weapon in a public place after threatening a security officer with a bread knife. In interview she stated that she had carried the knife in order to threaten but not to injure. This story was perfectly consistent with the evidence of other witnesses and the police were unable to shake the defendant's adherence to this story in interview.

It is also assumed that police interviewers are concerned to test or undermine any defence raised in interview which is not believed. This is not always the case. It is not uncommon for police interviewers to dismiss as not capable of belief a defence raised at interview which is later successful in court. Thus, in AHA65, the defendant had been seen drinking a bottle of wine in a shop, near the wine display. He was arrested for theft but asserted that he had been given the bottle of wine by an elderly lady whom he had helped move some furniture. This defence was vigorously asserted at the time of arrest but ignored by the police who decided that the evidence of shoplifting was so clear that it was unnecessary to hold a formal interview. In fact this defence was raised successfully in court and supported by various details about the time and place when the gift of wine had been made. The prosecution were in no position to counter this evidence, although it might have been possible to undermine or disprove this story had these details been elicited following arrest. This was a case in which the prosecution were effectively ambushed not by the defence, but rather by the failure of the police to take an opportunity to refute or confirm the defence put to them by the accused.

Acquittals where a new defence is raised at trial

This category includes 3 cases in which the defendant was acquitted following exercise of the right to silence which are considered in the next section. Other cases in which a new defences was raised for the first time at trial are considered in Chapter 5 *Ambush defences*.

Acquittals following exercise of the right to silence

The 3 cases in which the defendant secured an acquittal after exercising the right to silence during police interrogation confirm the view expressed above that in the absence of good independent evidence available prior to the interrogation it makes little difference whether the suspect denies the offence or says nothing.

In AHJ01, the suspect was arrested as one of a group of youths who were responsible for breaking a car window and stealing a valuable computer from the car. Another member of the group admitted the damage and the theft. J01 was seen in association with the other youths soon after the offences but was not seen at the scene of the crime. In the course of interview in the presence of his parents and a solicitor, J01 first denied any involvement and answered every subsequent question: 'nothing to say'. In court J01 admitted being in the vicinity and knowing that the computer had been stolen after the event, but denied direct involvement in either offence. Nothing that he said in court was inconsistent with the prosecution evidence. He was acquitted because the court did not accept that guilt could be inferred from the circumstantial evidence offered by the prosecution. It is very doubtful whether the police would have gained any advantage from J01 answering further questions in interview. He did not deny the factual basis of the prosecution case, and there was no direct evidence of involvement which could have been put to him in interview in order to shake his denial.

Similar reasoning applies to CEA113. Following a car search the police found a decorated rounders bat. When interviewed about this A113 answered 'No comment' to all questions. At his trial for possession of an offensive weapon, the defence argued that the bat was not offensive *per se* and that therefore the defendant must be acquitted in the absence of proof of an intent to use the bat to injure. This argument was accepted by the magistrates' court and A113 was acquitted. Had A113 answered questions it seems unlikely that he would have admitted that he had the bat for an offensive purpose. Since there was no independent evidence of this it is difficult to see on what basis the police might have undermined this defence.

In the third silence case, ATJ22, it is probable that there was sufficient evidence to secure a conviction whatever the defendant's attitude in interview, and that the case failed because the prosecution chose an inappropriate charge. The defendant had been seen in the back seat of a BMW motor car which had a smashed window. When arrested later he was found to be in possession of some broken spark plug insulator (notoriously used for breaking car windows). In the course of arrest and being conveyed to the police station he was alleged to have made incriminating admissions but was later certified by a police surgeon to be too drunk to be interviewed. He was released on police bail to return to the police station two days later. When interviewed on that occasion, after consulting a solicitor, he answered no comment to all questions. J22 was acquitted on charges of criminal damage and going equipped for theft after the police officers who allegedly received his admissions were discredited. However, prosecuting counsel pointed out to a researcher that although there was no evidence that the defendant had broken the car window, there would have been sufficient evidence to sustain a conviction on a charge of interfering with a motor vehicle.

Summary

The view that a large number of acquittals (including dropped cases) result from defendants exploiting favourable procedural rules or conning gullible juries is not borne out by the present findings. In two thirds of cases in which a defendant avoids conviction this is the result of the CPS dropping the case rather than a jury verdict after a contested trial. More than a quarter of all acquittals are on policy grounds or because of some technical difficulty. In the great majority of cases which were dropped for insufficient evidence or in which the defendant was acquitted after trial, the defendant had raised a defence in police interview. In only 8 cases (10 per cent of all acquittals) did the defendant secure an acquittal after exercising the right to silence. In the majority of these cases the evidence was weak. Had the suspect been induced to speak and had then incriminated himself, it might have been possible to obtain a conviction. However, it was not clear that there would have been any clear advantage to the police if the defendant had chosen to deny the allegations in interview rather than remaining silent.

5. AMBUSH DEFENCES

One of the major concerns of those who advocate modification or abolition of the right to silence in police interview, is that the right permits a defendant to raise an 'ambush defence' at trial. In this context the term 'ambush defence' is taken to mean a defence which is raised for the first time at trial and of which the police or prosecution had no prior notice. It has been argued that by reserving his defence until trial the defendant gains an unnecessary and unfair advantage by depriving the police of the opportunity to investigate it and thereby disabling the prosecution from effectively refuting the defence in court.[1]

Restrictions on the right to ambush in current law

At present a judge may tell the jury that in assessing what weight to give to a defence they may take into account the fact that it was first put forward at trial[2] but the judge must be wary not to suggest or hint that the jury may infer guilt from the defendant's failure to mention the defence to the police.

In the limited context of alibi defences the scope for raising an ambush defence has been curtailed by statute. By section 11 of the Criminal Justice Act 1967, relating to trials on indictment, the accused is required to give notice of an alibi defence which he wishes to rely upon at trial. Failure to do so may result in the trial judge refusing to admit the alibi evidence at trial or admitting it subject to comment about the lack of the required notice. In practice it would be rare for a judge to refuse to allow an asserted defence to go before the jury.

Proposals for reform

The recommendations of both the CLRC and the Home Office Working Group and the new legislation, effective in Northern Ireland since December 1988, address the perceived problem of ambush defences. Under the CLRC's proposals a court or jury would be entitled to draw

---

[1] Criminal Law Revision Committee (1972), para 30. In announcing the setting up of the Home Office Working Group, the Home Secretary, Mr. Hurd stated: "I am not convinced that the protection which the law now gives to the accused person who ambushes the prosecution can be justified" (Hansard, 18 May 1988).
[2] Gilbert [1977] 66 Cr App R 237. For a discussion of the relevant case law see Easton (1991), pp. 9–16.

whatever inferences appear proper where in the course of interview or on being charged, the accused failed to mention any fact which he later relied upon at trial.[3] Under the Committee's proposals, the formal requirement of a caution before interrogation would be abolished on the basis that it provides 'an excuse for keeping back a false story until it becomes difficult to expose its falsity'.[4] Under the proposals however the police would be required to advise an accused after being charged to mention any fact which he intends to rely upon in his defence, since if such fact is held back it would be less likely to be believed and might have a bad effect on his case in general.[5]

The Home Office Working Group adopted the CLRC proposal in a modified form to provide greater safeguards for the suspect. The Group proposed that statutory guidelines should be issued relating to the factors which might be taken into account in drawing inferences from the accused's failure to disclose his defence. A new caution would be introduced warning the accused that his refusal to answers questions would be recorded; that it would be best to mention any fact on which he proposed to rely in his defence, and that if he witheld his defence, it would be less likely to be believed at trial.[6]

Clause 3 of the Criminal Evidence (Northern Ireland) Order 1988 permits the drawing of adverse inferences against an accused person who unreasonably failed to mention to the police any fact relied upon in his defence in court. The reform follows the recommendations of the CLRC except that under the Code of Practice issued under the Northern Ireland Police and Criminal Evidence Order 1989, a suspect must be cautioned that a failure to mention any fact relied upon in support of a defence in court, may be treated as supporting any evidence against the accused. Contrary to the proposals of the CLRC, this caution should be administered prior to interview and again prior to charge.

Identifying ambush defences

Although many commentators are willing to assume that ambush defences present a substantial problem, there has been little attempt to define what is meant by the term. Before any attempt is made to quantify ambush defences it is first necessary to identify the essential characteristics of an ambush defence and the circumstances in which such a defence may arise.

---

[3] Cl. 1 Draft Criminal Evidence Bill appended to Criminal Law Revision Committee (1972).
[4] Criminal Law Revision Committee (1972) para 43.
[5] *Ibid* para 44.
[6] Home Office (1989), pp. 51–52.
[7] See for instance Easton (1991), p. 47.

The consensus among commentators appears to be that ambush defences exhibit the following characteristics.[7]

i.   The defence is raised for the first time at trial or perhaps at committal.

ii. The defence takes the prosecution by surprise.

iii. The evidence or explanation on which the defence is based could have been given during police interrogation.

iv. The prosecution is hampered or prejudiced, either because investigation of the defence is made impossible or more difficult by lapse of time, or because the prosecution has insufficient time to prepare its case in the light of the new defence.

v.   The accused may be unfairly advantaged because he has time to perfect his story or prepare witnesses or other evidence.

vi. The risk of wrongful acquittal is greater than would have been the case had the defence been disclosed at the earliest opportunity.

vii. The defence is false.

It is not clear that all commentators would restrict the ambush category to false defences. A perfectly true defence which is not disclosed until trial may inconvenience the prosecution and the courts and is wasteful of resources. However, if the central focus of the current debate is on the avoidance of unmerited acquittals, it is arguable that in considering the prevalence and effects of ambush defences, we should exclude defences which are true (where this is reliably verified).

It is also clear that a defence will not be considered an ambush merely because the accused fails to nominate the appropriate legal category of defence. Thus, the purpose of the reforms proposed by the CLRC and the Home Office Working Group and enacted in Northern Ireland, is to encourage the accused to mention the 'facts' to be relied upon in his defence, rather than the defence itself. This is sensible in that any defence must have a basis in both fact and law, and although the accused may have a common sense understanding of what factors might exculpate him, he is unlikely to be able to state the precise legal basis for his defence. The prosecution would not be prejudiced by this since it is part of a lawyer's skills to allocate facts to legal categories.

Classifying defences

A defence is any plea which if raised successfully in a criminal trial will lead to a complete acquittal. Defences take many forms and on analysis it becomes apparent that not all types of defence are capable of fulfilling the criteria of ambush set out above. What follows is a consideration of the various types of defence which may be raised in a criminal trial in order to determine which sorts of defence may be classified as ambushes. In a number of cases whether or not a defence in a particular category amounts to an ambush defence, will turn upon whether the accused relies upon 'ambush facts' – ie facts which could have been mentioned in the course of police interview but were not in fact disclosed.

i. Claims that the conduct alleged by the prosecution does not amount to an offence known to the law

A defence of this sort does not involve any challenge to the factual basis of the prosecution case. It is not a defence which the accused could be expected to raise in interrogation. In formal terms there can be no element of surprise since in all cases it is the function of the prosecutor to satisfy himself or herself that the conduct alleged amounts to an offence. Also, there can be no question of the prosecution being prejudiced if this defence is raised at a late stage in the proceedings since a court should permit an adjournment where the parties need to prepare for a complex legal argument, and the 'investigation' required would relate to available legal sources. Thus, a defence of this sort can never be considered an ambush.

ii. Procedural defences which lead directly to acquittal

A number of procedural defences lead directly to acquittal if successful. Examples are a plea that the accused has been either acquitted or convicted of substantially the same offence on another occasion and a plea that the prosecution is an abuse of the court's process. There will be no question of an ambush defence where the basis of the plea would not have been apparent to the accused without legal advice. It will also not be an ambush where the primary facts are not in dispute and the ultimate issue depends upon a judgmental assessment of those facts (eg a plea that the prosecution should be dismissed for excessive delay).

A procedural defence might fall into the ambush category if it was supported by ambush evidence (as defined above) and the accused had appreciated the relevance of this evidence at the time of his interview with the police.

iii. Procedural defences which lead indirectly to acquittal

This category includes challenges to the admissibility of prosecution evidence (eg a challenge to the admissibility of an alleged confession under sections 76 or 78 PACE Act) which if successful might lead to the collapse of the prosecution case. Where such a challenge is based upon the circumstances of the police interview or other interactions with the police which preceded it, the defence should not be considered an ambush even if the issue is raised first at trial. The reason for this is that in all cases the prosecution should be prepared to establish the admissibility of its own evidence. The police officers who attended the interview should be prosecution witnesses to prove the alleged confession. If issues are raised about what took place in the interview room, these officers will be in as good a position as the accused to give evidence about what occurred. Thus, there is no question of the prosecution being obstructed by the defence being raised for the first time at trial.

In the circumstances under consideration the defendant could not be expected to raise the procedural defence in the course of interview. The procedures for ruling evidence inadmissible in sections 76 and 78 PACE operate to remedy misconduct by police in the course of interview. A suspect should not be expected to raise his objection to the procedures being adopted in the course of the interview in question.

iv. A simple denial of an element of the offence

In a criminal trial the burden of proof rests on the prosecution to prove all the positive elements of the offence. There will be no ambush if the defendant simply denies one or more element of the offence without adducing particular evidence in support of this. In such cases the defence is simply to put the prosecution to proof of the offence.

v. A denial of an element of the offence supported by ambush evidence

It would be an ambush defence if the accused were to deny an element of the offence and support this with ambush evidence. An example of this would be where the accused denied the necessary intent and claimed that at the relevant time his perception of the consequences of his acts had been affected by some drug which had been administered to him without his knowledge.

vi. A defence proper

A defence proper is a plea which can provide a defence in law notwithstanding that the prosecution have proved all of the positive elements of the offence. The most common example is the plea of self defence. Where such a defence is raised, some evidence must be adduced in its support in order to make it a live issue at trial. However, this may be no more than the defendant's own testimony. Once the defence has become an issue in the case the burden of disproving it beyond reasonable doubt is cast on the prosecution. A defence proper could amount to an ambush defence if supported by ambush evidence.

Circumstances in which a defence will not amount to an ambush

Even where a defence is raised for the first time at trial and falls within an appropriate category, it should not be considered as an ambush if any of the following conditions are satisfied:

i. the suspect is not given sufficient information about the suspicions against him to indicate the relevance of the facts on which his defence is later based;

ii. the suspect is not given an opportunity to put the factual basis of his defence in interview;

iii. the suspect is subjectively unaware of the potential for raising a defence.

Authoritative approaches to the classification of ambush defences

Official reports and commentators who have discussed ambush defences have tended to assume that the question of classification is self-evident and unproblematic. This is evident in the CLRC's Eleventh Report which does not define the term and gives a number of examples of defences which could amount to ambush. These are alibi, belief that goods were not stolen (on a charge of handling stolen goods), justifiable use of force (on a charge of robbery), consent (on a charge of rape) and innocent association (eg that the accused took a child into some bushes to show her a bird's nest, on a charge of indecency).[8]

It is accepted that defences of alibi, justifiable use of force and innocent association may be ambush defences. However, as argued, above the remaining two cases, consent in rape and lack of belief that goods were stolen, could amount to ambush defences only if supported by evidence not previously notified to the prosecution.

The incidence of ambush defences in the research sample

The incidence of ambush defences in the research sample was determined by analysing all cases in which the suspect was charged except for those cases in which the defendant pleaded guilty, or accepted a bind over in return for charges being dropped. The account of the trial was compared with the evidence on the prosecution file and other information about the case collected from the officers or prosecutors involved in it.

This sub-sample contained 113 cases, of which 34 resulted in guilty verdicts on one or more charge after trial. Of the 79 cases in which guilty

---

[8] Criminal Law Revision Committee (1972), para 33.

verdicts were not attained, in 25 cases the defendant was acquitted after a contested trial and in 54 cases the charges were dropped by the prosecution. The "dropped" category includes cases which were discontinued or withdrawn by the prosecution and also cases in which the defendant was found not guilty after the prosecution had offered no evidence.

The reason for including dropped cases in the sample is that in a system in which the outcome of many cases is determined without trial it must be recognised that a defence raised by an accused person may operate to secure an acquittal (or discontinuance or withdrawal) without the issue being tested before a court. This may occur where a defence lawyer intimates the nature of a defence at pre-trial review[9] or in discussions with the prosecutor in court. There is thus scope for ambush defences to operate prior to a full trial, for instance where a defence lawyer indicates that there is evidence to support a defence of which the police had no notice, and the CPS decide to drop the case because there is insufficient prosecution evidence to refute the defence raised.

Ambush defences in acquittals after contested trials

Contested trials were held in 59 cases. Acquittals were recorded in 25 (42 per cent) of these. In 17 cases the defence raised in court and the evidence on which it was based had been indicated previously to the police. In 8 cases (32 per cent of court acquittals) a defence was raised in court which had not been mentioned in police interview. In 3 of these cases the defendant had refused to answer some or all questions relating to his own involvement in the alleged offence.

In none of the 8 cases in which a new defence was raised in court could the defence be classified as an ambush according to the criteria suggested above. Two cases (AHJ49, BWA62) were dismissed at the request of the defence on grounds of excessive delay. As noted above, such a procedural defence cannot be classified as an ambush. In both cases the defence lawyer had indicated that if the case had proceeded the accused would have pleaded not guilty on the basis of the defence raised in police interview. The remaining 6 cases were as follows:

> AHJ01 The defendant was arrested in association with a group of youths one of whom admitted to breaking a car window and stealing a computer from the car. In interview J01 initially said that he had nothing to do with the incident and then answered all subsequent questions: 'Nothing to say'. At trial the prosecution case was simply that J01 was seen in the company of the principal offender soon after the offence. The judge

---

[9] Baldwin (1985).

rejected a defence submission of no case to answer. In the witness box J01 admitted being in the vicinity and knowing that the computer had been stolen, after the event. This testimony was perfectly consistent with the evidence called by the prosecution. J01 was acquitted.

BWJ16 The defendant had been found in possession of a knife. He admitted possession but denied having it for an offensive purpose. He was charged with possession of an offensive weapon: the prosecution case being that the knife was a flick knife and as such was 'offensive *per se*'. He was acquitted following a legal argument about whether the knife was or was not a flick knife.

BKA76 The defendant was arrested after being found blind drunk inside a market hall in the early hours of the morning, having activated the burglar alarm. In interview the interviewing officer referred throughout to A76 "breaking into" the market and did not follow up his statement that he had fallen in. The interview was terminated after the police persuaded him to accept the hypothetical proposition that if there had been something worth stealing in the building, he would have stolen it. At his trial for burglary he was acquitted after he gave evidence that he had accidentally walked on to the roof of the building and in his drunken state had fallen through a skylight. This story was plausible since the rear of the market hall adjoined a public park, and its roof was only three feet above the level of the ground in the park.

CCA27 The defendant was arrested at a scene of public disorder and charged with being drunk and disorderly. The police case was that he had interfered in their attempts to arrest others and that he had been shouting and swearing and inciting the crowd to attack the police. He was released after a period for sobering up but not interviewed. At trial, he claimed that he had been peacefully querying the reasons for arresting the other people and produced a witness who gave evidence to this effect. He was acquitted.

CEA113 In the course of searching the defendant's car for drugs, the police found a decorated rounders bat of a sort sold as souvenirs in Spain. A113 was arrested for possession of an offensive weapon. In interview A113 answered 'No comment' to all questions. In court it was held that there was no case to answer after the defence solicitor had successfully argued that the bat was not "offensive *per se*".

ATJ22 The prosecution case against J22 rested upon the fact that he had been seen inside a car and had allegedly made admissions to the officers who arrested him. His defence which was successful at court involved challenging the credibility of the officers who claimed to have received his admissions.

In none of these cases did the defence raised in court fulfil the criteria of an ambush set out above. In CCA27 and BKA76, there was no ambush because the defendant was not given an opportunity to put the factual basis of his defence in interview. In CCA27 there was no interview, whereas in BKA76, the defence was that A76 had not intended to enter the premises and did not intend to steal at the time of entry. The interviewing officer had asked no questions about these matters and had brushed aside A76's attempts to raise them.

In both BWJ16 and CEA113, the defence merely put the prosecution to proof that the thing in question was 'offensive'. This defence did not depend upon any evidence not already available to the prosecution but merely involved the proper characterisation of the thing found in the defendant's possession. Similarly in ATJ22 the defence involved a challenge to the credibility of the officers giving evidence for the prosecution. In AHJ01, the defence did not contradict any of the factual evidence presented by the prosecution, but merely pointed out that it did not amount to proof of the offences charged.

Ambush defences in dropped cases

Fifty four cases were dropped. In one case only did it appear that the reason for dropping was a new defence which had not previously been asserted.

AHJ38 A person had broken into a car. Some time later J38 was seen in the vicinity and identified by the car owner as the person who had broken into it. On the way to the police station he denied any knowledge of the offence. In interview he refused to answer any questions. J38 was charged with criminal damage and attempted theft. In court no evidence was offered after the defence solicitor indicated to the prosecutor that he intended to challenge the identification evidence.

There was no ambush in this case, the defence amounted to a simple denial of the offence and a challenge to the quality of the only piece of prosecution evidence.

Ambush defences in guilty verdicts

In 34 cases the defendant was found guilty following a contested trial of some or all charges. In 6 cases the defence raised in court had not (according to official records) been mentioned in the course of interview.

ATA27 The defendant was charged with burglary at a pub' after closing time. In interview A27 refused to answer questions, but later issued an alibi notice which stated that he had not been arrested in the pub, but rather he had been on the other side of the road sitting on a bench outside a busy mini-cab office. No apparent attempt was made to disprove this (for instance by seeking witnesses from the mini-cab office). In court A27 was convicted on the strength of the evidence of three police offices who gave evidence that he had been arrested in the pub.

ATA72 The defendant admitted hitting a process server who had come to serve an eviction notice on him. In the course of interview A72 said that 'He reached out to grab me, so I just hit him' and also denied knowing that the victim was an officer of the court. This answer was not followed up and subsequent questions related only to the extent of the assault. In court A72 unsuccessfully raised the defence of self-defence.

In neither of the above cases was the defence an ambush. ATA27 would have involved an ambush but for the alibi notice procedure. In ATA72, the defendant gave clear indications that he might claim self defence but was not given an opportunity to develop this claim in the course of the interview.

In one case the prosecution asserted that the defence had been heard for the first time in court, although this was not in fact the case.

CEA32 An ornamental garden wall had been damaged late at night. This had been witnessed by the householder. When A32 walked down the same street later that night he was identified as the perpetrator by the householder. In interview A32 denied the offence and said that he had walked down the same road earlier and had seen a group of four or five youths messing about near the wall. The police did not seek further details and did not ask A32 if he had seen any of these other youths damage the wall. At trial A32 gave evidence about the other group of youths and raised the defence that the householder had mistaken him for one of them. The only evidence against A32 was the identification by the householder at a distance in the dark. A32 was convicted following a prosecution closing address which (without objection by the defence) emphasised that the jury should be wary of believing the defendant's story which was heard for the first time in court.

In two cases, BWJ40 and ATA109 (discussed in the next section) it was not clear whether the defence raised in court was or was not an ambush because the defendant claimed to have asserted the defence or tried to do so in interview but this had been excluded from the record.

Only one case in this group involved a clear ambush defence.

CCA24 The defendant was present at scene of public disorder following a football match. He interceded to try and prevent the police arresting his brother but was pushed away by a PC. Some time later A24 visited the police station to enquire about his brother and was arrested for obstructing a police officer. In interview he answered 'No comment, no comment, no comment to anything you have to say'. At trial he argued that he had been simply querying his brother's arrest and that he had left the scene when pushed away by a police officer. The magistrates found the obstruction charge proved.

The problem of unanticipated defences

Of the 59 cases which were determined by contested trial, in 14 cases a defence was raised at trial which had not been fully expressed at interview. As indicated above, only between 1 and 3 of these cases involved true ambush defences.

In view of the relative rarity of true ambush defences it is perhaps strange that they are accepted in many quarters as presenting a significant problem for the criminal justice system, requiring solution by law reform. Part of the explanation may lie in the rather greater number of cases coming before the courts in which the defence raised is unanticipated by the prosecution, although not amounting to an ambush.

As argued in the first section of this Chapter, certain types of defence (eg defences based on points of law and procedural defences) are necessarily raised for the first time in court, and the prosecution will not be prejudiced when this occurs. However, the research sample contains a number of cases in which the prosecution were wrong-footed by a defence raised for the first time in court, not amounting to an ambush, but of a sort which could have been raised at interview.

The explanation for such unanticipated defences relates to the fact that in an adversarial system the function of the police is to construct a case for the prosecution. The primary means of constructing the prosecution case is the interview. The desired product of the interview is an unambiguous confession, free of internal contradictions. The police understand the power of such a confession: when presented to the defence solicitor on disclosure of the prosecution case it may prompt the lawyer to advise a guilty plea; presented in court it may secure a guilty verdict. A corollary of this is that the police cannot afford to allow the interview to become a platform for the accused person's defence. It is therefore important that the interviewer exercises careful control of the agenda of the interview. To this end the police interviewer may effectively ignore any hint of a defence raised by the suspect and cut short any attempt at exculpation. The operative assumption is that the suspect is guilty and any attempt to contradict this must be a lie. Thus, in cases where the defendant raises a defence in court for the first time, the fact that the matter was not explored at interview may be the result of police interrogation technique rather than of an attempt by the defendant to withhold the defence.

This was the case in CEA32, (discussed above) in which prosecuting counsel discredited the accused before the jury by claiming that he had told one story to the police and another one in court, whereas his testimony in court had been entirely consistent with what he said in interview. If it is assumed that prosecuting counsel was not deliberately misleading the court, the most likely explanation for the error is that because the suspect's asserted defence was summarily brushed aside at interview, prosecuting counsel perhaps skimming the file, missed it. From the point of view of the prosecution this was in effect an ambush, but one laid by the police not the defendant.

Further examples of the police exercising control of the interview to construct out all but the faintest hints of exculpation are BKA76 and ATA72 which are discussed above.

There is also some evidence in this study that in some cases a defence asserted by the accused to the police, was excluded from the formal record. The defence lawyer argued that this was the case in BWJ40. In this case a sixteen year old girl in the care of a local authority had made a hoax telephone call to the fire brigade. At trial she admitted that she had made the call but pleaded that she had done so under duress from two other girls. Although there was no mention of this in the formal record of interview, J09 claimed that she had told the interviewing police officer that the other girls knew that she was making the telephone call, but that the social worker present had intervened and said that the other girls did not know about the telephone call and that the police officer had written down the social worker's reply and not the reply originally made by J40. There is some support for this account in the contemporaneous note of interview.

PC: "So at the time of the call you were on your own and the other two did not know what you were doing?".

J40: "Yes".

Two things may be noted about this statement which exculpated the other two girls: first, it appears to refer to some earlier discussion of the issue although none is recorded in the contemporaneous note; secondly, the statement was constructed by the police officer. Although, it is common for police officers to construct statements for suspects,[10] such police constructed statements normally tend to incriminate either the interviewee or another. This case is unusual in that the police constructed statement tends to exculpate the other girls. This case therefore appears at odds with our normal understanding of police interview techniques. If however, as J40 later alleged, the purpose of this interchange was to exclude the possibility of a duress defence, it would be completely consistent with other accounts of police interview techniques.

ATA109, was another case in which according to official accounts, a defence was raised for the first time in court. The prosecution case rested upon evidence of a police officer that he had seen the defendant trying car door handles, that the defendant had been holding a half brick but had dropped it when the police officer approached, and that the defendant had made various admissions at the time of arrest. In court the defendant denied making the alleged admissions and claimed to have given explanations for a screwdriver, gloves and tape which were found in his possession. He also denied possession of the brick and said that he had first seen it when the arresting PC showed it to him after his arrest. Interestingly, when interviewed by a researcher soon after the incident, the officer also stated that the defendant had denied possession of the brick. However, this was contradicted by the officer's evidence on the police file and in court.

The defendant was charged with going equipped for theft and with interfering with motor vehicles. The going equipped charge was dropped on resource grounds after the defendant elected Crown Court trial. He was however convicted on the interfering with vehicles charge in the magistrates court.

What is remarkable about ATA109 is that although A109 was found in possession of incriminating articles and was detained for a total of ten hours, no formal interview ever took place. It was hardly satisfactory to rely upon vague, incomplete and uncorroborated admissions recorded only in the arresting officer's notebook. Although the defendant's explanation for his possession of the incriminating articles was given for

---

[10] McConville et al (1991), Chap 4, in which the relevant literature is reviewed.

the first time at trial (at least according to the official account) this was a conequence of a police decision not to give him the opportunity to raise it in interview.

Summary

This study indicates that the common perception that ambush defences pose a significant problem for the criminal justice system, may be erroneous. In particular it is argued that many types of defence which may be raised in the course of a criminal trial cannot amount to ambushes. Of the 59 contested trials examined there was only one clear case of an ambush defence, and two other cases in which the prosecution claimed that there had been an ambush but this was in effect contested by the defence. The proportion of contested cases in which ambush defences were raised was therefore at most 5 per cent. This study also discloses a problem of defences which are raised in court but which are unanticipated as a consequence of police interrogation tactics designed to exclude exculpatory statements from the record. The study discloses between 3 and 5 of such unanticipated defences, amounting to up to 8.5 per cent of the total sample of contested cases.

6. POLICE RESPONSES TO DEFENCES RAISED IN INTERVIEW

One of the arguments raised in support of the abolition or modification of the right to silence is that it is advantageous for both the prosecution and the innocent suspect if the suspect answers questions and indicates any defence which he wishes to raise in the course of interview. The advantage to the prosecution is said to be that the police have the opportunity to test the story told by the suspect in the course of interview and also to carry out further investigations in order to confirm or refute it. In relation to cases which go to trial, it is also advantageous that the suspect has disclosed his defence because this makes it more difficult to raise any defence at trial which is inconsistent with what was said at interview.

The advantage to the innocent suspect lies in the opportunity to put his defence. This enables the police to investigate the defence raised and where it is confirmed to eliminate the suspect from the inquiry at an earlier rather than a later stage.[1]

These arguments rest upon a number of assumptions about police interviews and police investigation. These assumptions are:

i.   that one of the purposes of police interview is to elicit the suspect's defence;

ii.   that as a matter of fact police interviews elicit suspects' defences;

iii. that where a defence is raised, this may be tested effectively in the course of interview;

iv.   that where a defence is raised the police have the opportunity to confirm or refute it by further investigation;

v.   that as a matter of fact the police conduct further investigations in order to confirm or refute defences raised in interview.

The purpose of the present study is to test these assumptions.

---

[1] Criminal Law Revision Committee (1972), para 4.3 (1). In his address to the Police Foundation in July 1987 the Home Secretary suggested that the interests of the innocent suspect would 'generally lie in a answering questions frankly'.

The case sample

This study involved a sample of 314 cases in which a defence was asserted by the suspect at some stage in the course of formal or informal interview with the police. Of the 848 suspects who were formally interviewed 37 per cent raised a defence. For this purpose asserting a defence is taken to include a simple denial. Cases in which the suspect was completely silent are excluded but cases in which the suspect was silent for part of the interview but also clearly denied the offence or asserted a defence at some stage, are included. Also excluded are a substantial number of cases in which the suspect denied the offence which was put to him but admitted or did not deny an alternative offence. Thus in one case the suspect who was accused of stealing a moped, told the police that he had not stolen it but had bought it for £15 knowing it to be stolen. The suspect then explained to the interviewing officer that this amounted to handling stolen goods rather than theft.

More commonly, the admission related to an offence of lesser gravity than the offence for which the suspect was initially arrested. In many such cases the response of the police and CPS was to proceed for the admitted offence even where this was considerably less serious than the offence for which the suspect was arrested. In some cases this resulted from a bargain by which the prosecution agreed to proceed on a lesser charge in return for a guilty plea. This occurred in CEA83, in which the CPS dropped a charge of assaulting a police officer and substituted a charge of obstruction, where the suspect had made statements consistent with obstruction in the course of vigorously denying the assault.

Perhaps surprisingly, this sample does not include all of the cases which terminated with a decision to take no further action. The reason for this is that in a number of cases suspects were released without further action before being given an opportunity to assert a defence. This occurred in relation to the following groups of suspects:

  i.   passengers in cars where it was suspected that the car had been taken without consent. In these cases it was common to interview only the driver and to release the passengers once the driver's claim to have authority to drive had been verified;

  ii. rape suspects who were arrested or brought to the police station purely for the purpose of providing an intimate sample, but who were not interviewed;

  iii. cases involving alleged public order offences in which the source of evidence was the police and it was considered unnecessary to interview the suspect;

iv. cases in which suspects were arrested in a group and released without interview after another member of the group had taken responsibility for the offence.

The Study

Each case was analysed in terms of the whether or not the interviewer had tried to break down the asserted defence in the course of interview, and the success of this tactic; whether or not there was a realistic opportunity to pursue further investigations in the light of the interview; whether or not such investigations were actually undertaken.

For the purposes of the present study no attempt was made to analyse the text of interviews to determine the tactics used to break down the suspect's asserted defence.

The judgement of whether or not there was a realistic opportunity to pursue further investigations was made by the researcher. In some cases this judgment was informed by a discussion of this issue in recorded interviews with police officers or prosecutors. A realistic opportunity for further investigation was taken to mean a line of inquiry which was indicated by the interview or other evidence in the case.

The sample was also analysed in terms of outcome and (where appropriate) plea. The group of cases in which there was a decision to take no further action were further classified according to whether or not the police were satisfied that the suspect was innocent.

The dynamics of the interview

Eliciting the suspect's defence

This study indicates that a large proportion of suspects managed to raise a defence. The study also identifies some cases in which an examination of the recorded interviews, other evidence in the file, and interviews conducted by researchers with police officers suggests that the suspect wished to raise a defence but was not given an opportunity to do so. Apart from this group of cases, it is possible that the larger sample of 1080 cases contains cases in which the suspect wished to raise a defence in interview but failed to do so. The research methods used would not be capable of discovering these cases. For these reasons it is not possible to quantify cases in which the police did or did not elicit a defence which the suspect wished to raise. However, an examination of interview records in cases in which a defence was asserted casts some light on the inclination and ability of the police to elicit defences in the course of interview.

Attempts to break down the suspect's defence in interview

The police interviewer attempted to break down the suspect's defence in 296 (94 per cent) of the 314 cases in which a defence was asserted. This met with complete success in 12 cases and partial success in 4 cases.[2] Thus police attempts to break down the suspect's defence met with some degree of success in only 16 cases (5.4 per cent). In 18 cases (6 per cent) there was no discernible attempt to question the defence raised in the course of interview.

The high rate of failure to break down the suspect's defence contradicts the often expressed view of the highly coercive interview environment in which only the toughest experienced criminal can withstand the pressure to drop his defence. Three explanations can be offered for the high failure rate: first, as indicated in Chapter 3, many defences are inscrutable, in the sense of providing no basis for logical dispute or refutation by counter evidence; secondly, because the police are rightly confident of obtaining convictions in many of these cases they do not go to extreme lengths to test suspects' stories; thirdly, for unexceptional cases, the police are not particularly concerned if they are unable to collect sufficient evidence to charge.

Inscrutability

Failure to break down a denial or defence asserted in interview may be explained by the absence of a basis on which the suspect's story may be attacked. Thus in BWA43, the defendant had admitted entering a school at night but claimed that he had done so only to mess around. In the absence of any direct evidence of intent to steal, the police interviewer could only express incredulity at the suspect's account. This case was subsequently dropped for lack of evidence. A similar problem arises in cases where the defendant is charged with assault but claims self defence. If, as is frequently the case, the only witnesses are the defendant and his alleged victim, the police may be faced with a stark clash of evidence, with nothing to indicate which should be believed and thus every incentive for the defendant to stick to his story whether true or not.

Confidence in obtaining a conviction

For many types of case the police have a reasonable expectation of obtaining a conviction notwithstanding the suspect's denial or defence at interview. Thus in 47 of the 65 cases in which the defendant either pleaded guilty or was convicted after trial, the police had been completely unsuccessful in breaking down his defence. This was the case in a number

---

[2] The low success rate for breaking down the suspect's defence in interview is consistent with the findings of Moston *et al* (1992A), and Baldwin (1992).

of shoplifting cases in which the defence was lack of intent. Thus in both BWA106 and CCA63, the defendant took goods from a shop without paying for them. In both cases the police interviewer doubted the story offered and attempted to persuade the defendant that what had occurred was theft as a matter of logic. In both case the defendant maintained the defence and pleaded not guilty in court, but was convicted.

Police confidence in obtaining a conviction may be justified even where the quantity of evidence is not great. Convictions frequently follow where the only evidence against the defendant is that of a single witness, who is of good character and who has no apparent motive for lying.

> *AHJ20* A witness had seen J20 apparently in the company of another youth who had smashed a car window and run away. J20 was apprehended by the witness and was later arrested by the police. He denied knowing the other boy and any involvement in the incident, but was convicted after denying the offence in the Juvenile Court.

In some such cases the defendant pleaded guilty after strenuously denying the offence in interview.

> *CEA90* A citizen saw A90 staggering down a street late at night, apparently drunk and damaging aerials and windscreen wipers on a succession of cars. He was followed to a house where he was later arrested by the police. Although he denied the offence completely in interview, A90 later pleaded guilty to criminal damage in the magistrates' court.

In some cases the police are content to leave the suspect's story untested because they consider that it bolsters the chances of a conviction.

> *BKA84/89* The two defendants were charged with assaulting the manager of a store. In interview they both admitted hitting the manager, but claimed that they did so in self-defence because of the degree of force he was using to eject them from the store. Although this story was expressed as a defence, the police interviewer would have been well aware that this evidence could also support the prosecution case by indicating a potential lawful justification for the manager's use of force against the defendants.

> *BWA25* The defendant was found late at night carrying bolt cutters, torch and gloves. He admitted that he had seen some scrap metal and had decided to steal it, but denied that he was carrying the equipment for this purpose. Technically, this denial raised a defence to the charge of going equipped for

theft. The police interviewer did not test this story, taking the view that the defence would be unlikely to stand up in court.

Lack of concern to charge

It is frequently assumed that the police are highly motivated to charge suspects and gain convictions and that this is reflected in vigorous interview tactics designed to break down any defence offered. This picture is however unrealistic. Whereas there are cases in which the police consider it important to charge and convict a particular offender, there are many others in which the police are not particularly concerned. Such a case was BKA102. The defendant had been named by an accomplice as being a member of a petrol siphoning gang. At the time of A102's arrest, the officers involved had already obtained confessions from two other members of the gang and were pleased with the investigation. A102's interview was terminated after fifteen minutes without any attempt being made to test his denials of involvement and his claim that he was elsewhere on the evening in question. It was apparent that having secured two likely convictions for the offences, the police were not particularly concerned whether they secured a third.

No attempt to break down the suspect's defence at interview

Of the 18 cases in which the police made no discernible attempt to break down the suspect's defence at interview, 14 were cases in which the police ultimately took no further action being satisfied of the suspect's innocence. In many cases these involved a speculative arrest on circumstantial evidence. A typical case is CEJ05. The suspect was named by two older boys as being in the vicinity when the older boys committed a burglary. In interview, the two other boys indicated that J05 had no positive role in the offence and J05 was released following a short interview in which he confirmed this. Similarly in BWA70/71/72, a police station window had ben smashed and three men walking past were arrested. A70 admitted the offence. A71 and A72 were released after brief interviews in which they confirmed that A70 was wholly responsible.

Further investigations

Of the 302 cases in which a defence was asserted and not broken down in the course of interview, there was a realistic opportunity to conduct further investigations in 102 cases (34 per cent) and no realistic opportunity to conduct further investigations in 200 cases (66 per cent).

In about two thirds (65) of the cases in which there was an opportunity for further investigation this was directly related to the text of the interview, whereas in about one third (37) the opportunity for further investigation arose independently of what was said in interview.

Of the 102 cases in which there was an opportunity to conduct further investigations, these were undertaken in 68 cases (67 per cent), but not in 34 cases (33 per cent). In relation to the 65 cases in which the opportunity to conduct further investigations related to the text of the interview, such further investigations were carried out in 45 cases (69%) and not carried out in 20 cases (31 per cent).

No opportunity to conduct further investigations

The figures above do not substantiate the assumption that in most cases where a suspect is induced to assert a defence at interview, this will enable the police to conduct further investigations to confirm or refute the denial made or defence raised. Analysis of the case sample suggests that for certain categories of case, notably where the suspect pleads either lack of intent or self-defence, there is normally little opportunity for further investigation.

Opportunity for further investigation independent of the text of the interview

In 37 cases the opportunity to conduct further investigations to confirm or refute the suspect's story in interview existed independently of the text of the interview. The following are a two examples.

> *AHA81* A window was broken at a wine bar to which A81 had recently been refused entry. A witness told the police that A81 had smashed the glass with his elbow. In interview A81 denied the offence but the police examined his jacket and found a sliver of glass embedded in the fabric. This investigation could have been carried out whether A81 denied the offence or was silent.

> *ATA20* A20 was arrested on suspicion of a stabbing after being recognised in a pub by the victim. In view of his denials the police organised an identity parade for two other witnesses to the attack. The identity parade could have been staged whether A20 denied the offence or was silent.

Opportunity for further investigation relates to the interview

In 65 cases the opportunity to conduct further investigation arose out of the interview. Here are a few examples.

> *ATA07/8* A van driver and a storeman employed by a car windscreen supplier were found to have loaded some screens into the firm's van without authorization. They were charged with theft and claimed that they had mistaken Jaguar windscreens for other screens and had loaded too many screens by mistake. On the advice of CPS evidence was taken from the

depot manager relating to the firm's procedures in order to refute the defence of mistake, and an employee was called as a witness with the screens in question in order to demonstrate that the alleged mistake relating to the Jaguar windscreen would not have been very likely.

ATJ48 Some drugs were found in the pocket of a jacket belonging to J48 while it was being worn by another boy. In interview, J48 denied that he knew anything about the drugs and suggested that his sister had worn the jacket recently and would have known if there were any drugs in it. The police checked with the sister who said that she had looked through the pockets for a hospital appointment card and no drugs had been present. No further action was taken for lack of evidence.

Further investigations undertaken

In two thirds of the cases in which there was a clear opportunity to conduct further investigations, such investigations were undertaken. The cases of AHA81, ATA20, ATA07/08 and ATJ48, discussed above are examples of this. The further investigation may be instrumental in securing a conviction or a decision to take no further action or to drop a case where the suspect had already been charged.

Generally, the police were most likely to conduct further investigations where these were relatively simple and straightforward. For instance, in CCA81 the police refuted a defence that A81 had damaged a nightclub door accidentally, by procuring a security video film from the club which clearly indicated that A81 had acted deliberately. In BWJ44, the names of schoolboy cross-country runners who might have witnessed the offence, were obtained by telephoning the Headmaster of the school. In a number of cases the necessary further enquiry related to a person who has attended the police station in relation to the suspect, typically a friend or parent who could be asked to confirm the suspect's story. This was the case in ATJ48 discussed above.

No further investigation undertaken

In one third of the cases for which it would have been possible to conduct further investigations no such investigations took place. These tended to be cases in which the necessary further investigation would have been more complex or time consuming. In some cases the suspect escaped prosecution simply by raising a plausible defence. Where this occurs the police may give the suspect the benefit of the doubt without any attempt to investigate the defence raised outside the interview room.

CEA15 The suspect was seen working with a set of ladders by X, who had recently had a similar set of ladders stolen. When interviewed A15 claimed to have bought the ladders six months previously and named a number of premises at which he said that he had worked using the ladders. A15 was released without charge and no attempt was made to check the defence raised.

CEA105 A man had stolen some goods from a shop and escaped on a motorcycle which was traced to A105. A105 also fitted the general description of the thief given by the shopkeeper. However, he strenuously denied the theft and claimed to have lent his motorcycle to another man whose identity he did not know. A105 was released without further investigation, and in particular without holding any form of identification procedure.

As the two cases discussed above illustrate, the police may neglect enquiries which are potentially advantageous to the prosecution as well as lines of enquiry which might exculpate the suspect.

In some cases in which the police neglect a line of inquiry indicated by the interview, they hope to gain a conviction without the further evidence, and in some cases are successful in doing so. In BKA27, the defendant was arrested and convicted for assault arising out of a fracas outside a fish and chip shop. Although the defendant admitted hitting the victim he claimed that he did so in self-defence and named a witness who could support his side of the story. The officer dealing with the case told a researcher that there was no need for more witnesses since the police already had five or six to say that A27 did it.

However, in other cases a potential conviction is lost as a result of a failure to follow up inquiries indicated by the interview. This was the case in BWA88. The door to a house had been damaged while A88 had been trying to gain entry. In interview he claimed that his knee had gone through the door when he slipped on the step leading up to it. The police officer conducting the interview expressed incredulity at the story but otherwise ignored it. At trial A88 raised this defence and was found not guilty. After the acquittal the officer described A88 as having fooled the court, because it would have been impossible to have damaged the door in the manner described by the defendant. However, no attempt had been made to pre-empt the anticipated defence by means of photographs or measurements of the door and the step.

Where the police fail to investigate a defence raised in interview, this may be because they are naturally sceptical of defences and may assume concoction. However, this approach may leave the prosecution open to ambush in court. This occurred in AHA65. The defendant had been seen drinking from a bottle of wine near to the wine counter in a supermarket. On arrest he claimed that he had been given the bottle of wine on an earlier occasion by an elderly lady whom he had helped by moving some furniture. The police treated the case as being so straightforward that no formal interview was held. In court the defendant raised the same defence and was found not guilty. The evidence which he gave included some details which the police might have been able to check, had the defence been elicited at interview.

In CCJ47/48 similar factors led to the case being dropped by the CPS. Two boys had been seen in the Gents lavatory at a roller skating rink changing wheels on skates which were owned by the rink. They were arrested for theft. Both denied this and claimed that they were changing the wheels temporarily for two girls who had been having difficulty with the wheels on the skates hired from the rink. Both boys stuck to this story even though the police interviewer tried to undermine it by pointing out illogicalities. No attempt was made to follow up the story about the girls. However, before the case came to trial the defence solicitor wrote to the CPS indicating that he had taken statements from the two girls which confirmed the story raised in interview. As a result the case was dropped by the CPS.

Summary

It has been assumed that it is advantageous to the police for the suspect to raise any defence at interview because this provides an opportunity to break down the defence by interrogation techniques. This study suggests that this advantage accrues in a relatively small proportion of cases. Whereas, the police attempted to break down the asserted defence in 296 out of 314 cases, this was successful or partially successful in only 16 cases (5.5 per cent of cases in which the police tried to break down the defence).

The assumption that the police are enabled to conduct further investigations if the suspect is induced to disclose his defence at interview is also not well founded. Of the 302 cases in which the suspect maintained his defence in interview, there were realistic opportunities to conduct further investigations in 102 cases (34 per cent). In 65 (22 per cent of the total cases in which a defence was maintained) cases the opportunity arose wholly or partly because of what was said at interview. Thus a realistic opportunity to conduct further investigations was generated by the interview in 22 per cent of cases.

Where there was opportunity to conduct further investigations to refute or confirm a suspect's defence, these were conducted in 65 out of

102 cases. Where the opportunity for further investigation was generated by the interview, further investigations took place in 45 of 65 cases.

Of the 314 cases in which the suspect initially raised a defence the interview was a source of advantage to the prosecution 61 cases (19%), comprising 16 cases in which the defence raised was wholly or partly broken down in the course of interview, and in the 45 cases in which the interview generated an opportunity for further investigation which was subsequently taken.

7. THE IMPLICATIONS FOR REFORM

The right to silence debate is conducted on many different planes. The range of arguments employed by both the proponents of reform and of those who would retain (or strengthen) the right, encompass both claims about fundamental constitutional values as well as sociological, psychological and utilitarian claims. Thus the proponents of reform base their case on:

i. *constitutional arguments* that the courts' primary concern should be accuracy in determining guilt or innocence, and courts should therefore hear all evidence logically suggestive of guilt; and further that citizenship duties should include a duty to co-operate with the criminal justice process;

ii. *sociological/psychological arguments* that silence in the face of an accusation is normally suggestive of guilt;

iii. *utilitarian arguments* that law reform would bring benefits in terms of more effectively convicting offenders.

Those who would retain the right, base their case on:

i. *constitutional arguments* that the state should not be able to require a citizen to answer questions, and that courts should be concerned not only with determining disputes accurately but also with the assertion and protection of citizens' rights;

ii. *sociological/psychological arguments* that silence in police interrogation may result from a complex of factors and is not necessarily indicative of guilt;

iii. *utilitarian arguments* about the risks of miscarriages of justice which might arise from unreliable admissions or confessions if suspects were placed under greater pressure to answer police accusations, and also about the dangers of convicting defendants on the basis of evidence of silence rather than on positive evidence of guilt.

A debate of this complexity could not be resolved by empirical research. However, the arguments of both sides rest on assumptions about the social meaning (and hence evidential value) of silence and the present workings of the criminal justice process, as well as predictions of the likely

71

effects of reform. Traditionally, the right to silence debate has been conducted on the basis of anecdote and experience. Over recent years a number of studies have cast light upon the extent of exercise of the right to silence (reviewed in Chapter 2 above) and the reliability of statements made in police interrogation. The purpose of the present research was to complement these earlier studies by testing some of the assumptions underlying arguments for reform. The findings are set out in the preceding Chapters. The function of this Chapter is to consider the implications of these findings for the reform debate.

Is silence evidence of guilt?

The arguments for reform rest upon a psychological assumption that the normal response of an innocent person when accused of crime is to deny it. This is linked to a sociological assumption that if suspects were to be isolated from positive influences to be silent (ie the present caution and legal advice) the major explanation for silence in police interrogation would be guilt. From this it is argued that where a suspect who had been silent in interrogation later raised a defence, the court would be justified in inferring that the defence was concocted (in effect an inference of guilt).

Until recently no evidence has been offered to support or contradict these assumptions. Where these assumptions have been considered on the level of theory and hypothesis, commentators have commonly fallen into the trap of confusing the question of whether silence may result from motives other than guilt, with the question whether such other motive would be reasonable or justifiable. As Greer has pointed out, such arguments are irrelevant.[1] If as a matter of fact there are motivations other than guilt for silence, then the force of the argument for drawing evidential inferences from silence is reduced accordingly.

However, whether guilt is the major motivation for silence is particularly difficult to test for two reasons. First, the very fact of silence makes it difficult to determine the suspect's motives. Secondly, since under present law the suspect must be cautioned that he need not answer, it clearly *cannot* be assumed that guilt is the motivation for silence. Whether or not silence could be treated as evidence of guilt if it followed a clear warning that silence might be equated with evidence (as proposed by the CLRC and Home Office Working Group) must be a matter of speculation.

Recent research has indicated that silence may be the product of a complex of factors unrelated to guilt (McConville, 1992; Baldwin, 1992). Whereas the present research was not designed to expose motivations for silence, it did produce evidence that shielding others may be a motivation

---

[1] Greer (1990), P.727.

in a small but significant number of cases. Although it is difficult to reliably quantify the extent to which factors other than guilt may be motivate silence, the very fact that such motivations can be identified substantially weakens the case for treating silence as evidence of guilt.

Would reform lead to the conviction of more offenders?

Whether or not reform would lead to the conviction of more offenders than are convicted under present arrangements, depends upon a number of inter-linked issues. These are:

    i.   whether the right to silence is exercised in a significant number of cases in which convictions are not obtained;

    ii.   whether a significant number of these cases fail for reasons which are not independent of the exercise of the right to silence;

    iii.   whether reform of the law as proposed would induce some otherwise silent suspects to speak;

    iv.   whether in such cases it would be advantageous to the prosecution for the suspect to answer questions rather than to remain silent;

and, in relation to suspects who would persist in silence notwithstanding the proposed caution:

    v.   whether any such cases would be likely to reach court; and

    vi.   whether in any such cases the prosecution would be better able to counter ambush defences, by virtue of being able to invite the jury to infer that the defence was concocted; and

    vii.   whether in cases in which the suspect was silent in both the police station and in court, adverse inferences could be drawn against him on the basis of his silence in the face of the prosecution case as presented in court.

Silent suspects who are not convicted

The right to silence was exercised by 4.5 per cent of suspects who were interviewed. About half of these were convicted. Thus, about 2 per cent of all suspects who were interviewed exercised the right to silence and escaped conviction.

The right to silence was exercised in about 4 per cent of cases which ended with no further action, and in about 10 per cent of cases which ended in acquittal (including cases in which charges were dropped before trial). This indicates that any reform of the law would have a potential impact on 2 per cent of all interviewed suspects, 4 per cent of NFA cases and 10 per cent of acquittals.

Do cases fail because of silence?

A major concern of the proponents of reform is that exercise of the right to silence contributes to suspects avoiding being charged, and charged suspects escaping conviction. This implies that a substantial proportion of such outcomes are unmerited and that higher charging and conviction rates might be achieved if the law were changed to increase the pressure on suspects to speak by permitting adverse inferences to be drawn from silence where the accused later raises a defence at trial.

The analysis of no further action decisions and acquittals in Chapters 3 and 4 indicates that it would be misleading to view all of such cases as negative outcomes, symptomatic of investigative failure. Thus, in over 60 per cent of cases which ended with no further action, the reason for the decision was one of policy, or because the victim withdrew the complaint, or because the police were satisfied that the suspect was innocent. Similarly, in 25 per cent of cases in which the suspect was prosecuted but a conviction was not obtained, the case was dropped prior to trial on grounds of policy or because of some technical problem unrelated to the evidence.

A number of cases failed following exercise of the right to silence (2 per cent of all suspects who were interviewed: 4 per cent of NFA cases: 10 per cent of acquittals and dropped cases). It is of course impossible to attribute such failures to silence since one can only speculate about what the result might have been had the suspect not exercised the right. However, a close analysis indicates that in a number of cases the operative reason for failure was independent of the suspect's silence. This was the case in 4 out of 9 silence cases which ended with a decision to take no further action. This suggests that the proportion of cases which might be affected by the reform proposals would be somewhat less than 4 per cent of NFA cases and 10 per cent of acquittals and dropped cases.

Would legal reform induce silent suspect's to speak?

Implicit in some of the arguments of the reformist lobby, is an assumption that by warning suspects of possible adverse consequences of silence, some suspects would be induced to speak who would not otherwise have done so. It would be impossible to test this assumption by empirical research unless the law were reformed as proposed and a before-and-after study conducted. Accordingly, there are no findings of the present study which bear directly on this issue. However, there is some indirect evidence which bears on the issue.

Under present arrangements suspects in custody have a right to receive legal advice and a right to have a solicitor present during interviews. There is evidence that in a substantial number of cases, police ploys to avoid the presence of a solicitor are successful, and that whether or not a solicitor is present may ultimately depend upon whether the solicitor (rather than the suspect) considers it necessary to attend.[2] However, in cases where the suspect does receive legal advice or a solicitor is present at interview, the solicitor may advise silence and this may prompt some suspects to not answer questions who otherwise would have done so.

The present study demonstrates a correlation between silence and the presence of a solicitor and prior legal advice. Whereas 10 per cent of all suspects who were interviewed had a solicitor present, 24 per cent of silent suspects were interviewed in the presence of a solicitor, and a further 18 per cent had received legal advice prior to interview. This correlation is confirmed by other recent studies conducted by the Metropolitan and West Yorkshire police forces (Home Office, 1989, Appendix C) and by Moston et al (1992B) and Baldwin (1992). It is impossible to determine the extent to which the presence of a solicitors or legal advice influences suspects to remain silent. However, recent research indicates that the extent to which lawyers advise silence is often exaggerated (Baldwin, 1992) and that the reasons for such advice may be complex. Indeed it is probable that in some cases the suspect requests a solicitor because he has already decided to remain silent. However, it is not unreasonable to assume that there is a causal link between advice and silence in *some* cases. If the law were reformed along the lines recommended by the CLRC or the Home Office Working Group, it seems likely that some solicitors who advise silence under present arrangements would advise suspects to speak. It would be also reasonable to assume that in some cases this advice would be followed.

However, it cannot be assumed that reform of the law as recommended by the CLRC and the Home Office Working Group would have a very marked effect on the numbers of suspects opting for silence. The proposed reform would appeal to the rationality of the suspect and his solicitor. It is argued that once adverse inferences could be drawn from silence, answering questions will become the rational choice of suspects who otherwise would have remained silent. But, clearly this will not always be the case. The prospect of adverse inferences being drawn would arise only if the case went to court. In many silence cases the suspect may

---

[2]. A. Sanders, L. Bridges, A. Mulvaney and G. Crozier (1989) *Advice and Assistance at Police Stations and the 24 Hour Duty Solicitor Scheme*, London, Lord Chancellor's Department; A. Sanders and L. Bridges 'Access to legal advice and police malpractice' [1990] Criminal Law Review 494.

realistically hope that the case will not reach court. For instance in 3 out of 5 cases in which charges were dropped after the suspect exercised the right to silence, the evidence was very weak. A suspect who is aware of the absence of evidence against him may realistically conclude that he has nothing to lose from silence.

Equally, where the evidence against a suspect is strong he may expect to be convicted (and will probably plead guilty) and therefore has nothing to lose from maintaining silence. It is notable that about a quarter of suspects who exercised the right to silence eventually pleaded guilty in court.

Is it necessary to place the suspect under further pressure to speak?

Under present law a suspect can be placed under considerable pressure to answer questions. Questioning may continue even though the suspect has indicated that he does not wish to answer questions. Where a first interview is unproductive the suspect may be detained within the time limits permitted by PACE for the purpose of second or subsequent interviews. The police may use vigorous and aggressive tactics provided that these fall short of what the courts would consider to be 'oppression' or likely in the circumstances to render unreliable any confession obtained.

The present research indicates that the police may not be fully utilising available tactics for overcoming silence. Thus, of the 49 cases in which the suspect was silent for some part of the interview, second or subsequent interviews were held in 6 cases (12 per cent). Of the 38 cases in which there was a significant exercise of the right to silence, there were repeat interviews in only 2 cases (5 per cent). It may be doubted whether there is a need to add to the means of putting pressure on suspects to speak, if in fact the police do not currently use all of the means available to them.

Is it advantageous to induce suspects to speak?

It is impossible to determine whether in particular cases the prosecution would have gained any advantage from inducing silent suspects to speak. However, some indication of the value of inducing suspects to speak in general, is provided by the study of police responses to defences raised at interview (Chapter 6). This indicates that the police were successful in breaking down defences raised at interview in only 5 per cent of the cases in which they attempted to do so; that 21 per cent of interviews presented a realistic opportunity for further investigations; and that further investigations related to the interview were actually carried out in 15 per cent of cases.

Qualitative analysis of cases involving denials, indicates that in many cases a denial is effectively as inscrutable as total silence and that this is particularly so where the independent evidence against the suspect is weak. Thus the suspect's denial was judged to be inscrutable in 75 per cent of cases which ended with no further action and in which the police were not satisfied of the suspect's innocence.

These findings suggest that the value of the interview in overcoming denials and providing opportunities for further investigation may be more mythical than real. Although cases do occur in which the police break down the suspect's defence or refute his story through further investigation, the absolute proportions of cases in which these occur is small.

Would more silence cases reach court if the law were reformed?

If the law were reformed as proposed by the CLRC or the Home Office Working Group, it is doubtful whether this would increase the likelihood of silent suspects being brought to court, or being committed for trial. A prosecution should be continued only if the Crown Prosecutor reviewing the case is satisfied that the evidence on the file indicates a realistic prospect of conviction. If the suspect had been silent at interview, the prosecutor would know that if a defence were to be raised in court, an inference might be drawn against the defendant. Equally the prosecutor would know that an inference of guilt might be drawn if the defendant remained silent in court in the face of solid prosecution evidence. However, the prosecutor could not rely upon the former type of inference to support the prosecution case, since, as indicated in Chapter 5, there a are many ways of defending a criminal charge in court without resorting to an ambush defence.

Equally, the strength of the prosecution case at the review stage could not be bolstered by anticipating that the defendant might remain silent in court and that the jury might draw an inference of guilt from this. The reason for this is that the prosecutor would have no way of knowing whether the defendant would maintain his silence in court. Under the reform proposals, a jury could be invited to infer guilt only where the defendant remained silent in court in the face of positive evidence against him.[3] If there were such evidence against the accused there would be no bar to proceeding with the prosecution and there would be no difficulty in getting the case committed for trial.

It is therefore not clear that reform of the law as proposed would substantially increase the number of cases going to trial.

---

[3] Criminal Law Revision Committee (1972), para 110, and *Draft Criminal Evidence Bill* appended to the Report, cl 5(1) (a); Home Office (1989), paras 113–114.

Would the proposed reform defuse ambush defences in court?

As indicated in Chapter 5, there is little evidence that ambush defences cause a significant problem for the criminal justice process. Where a suspect has remained silent in the police station, there are many ways of defending a criminal charge which do not involve ambushing the prosecution. In the research sample true ambush defences were raised in a maximum of 5 per cent of contested cases (convictions were recorded in all such cases).

A greater problem for the criminal justice system is the defence which is unanticipated by the prosecution but which does not amount to an ambush. Unanticipated defences result from the police practice of marginalising or ignoring defences which a suspect attempts to raise in interview. The consequences of these practices are that the prosecution have inadequate details of any defence to be raised and that investigations necessary to refute (or confirm) the asserted defence, are not conducted. Unanticipated defences figured in between 5 per cent and 8 per cent of contested cases.

Under the proposals of the CLRC and the Home Office Working Group the judge, prosecution and the defence would be empowered to comment on the accused's failure to mention any fact relied upon in his defence at trial. In particular the jury could be invited to infer that the defence was untrue. The numbers of ambush cases in the research sample are too small to permit a systematic consideration of how these proposals might operate. However, a number of factors suggest that the proposed reform would have little effect. First, the research provides no support for the belief that ambush defences lead to acquittals. Secondly, under present law the jury can be told that the defence has been raised for the first time in court and may draw whatever inferences they choose from this.[4] Thirdly, whatever the formal burden of proof, juries recognise that an accused person may have a motive for lying and will be sceptical of defences which are not supported by evidence other than the defendant's own word.

Would the proposed reforms increase the likelihood of convicting suspects who are silent in both the police station and court?

Under present law a judge, but not prosecuting counsel, may comment on an accused's failure to give evidence by pointing out to the jury that they have been deprived of the opportunity of hearing his story tested in cross examination.[5] Under the reform proposed by the CLRC, and incorporated into Article 4 of the Northern Ireland Order, the fact that a defendant does not give evidence may be dramatised by a procedure in

---

[4] *Raviraj* (1986) 85 Cr App R 93.
[5] *Bathurst* [1968] 2 QB 107; *Sparrow* [1973] 1 WLR 488.

which he is called upon to give evidence. If he declined to do so the jury would be able to draw whatever inferences appeared proper in the circumstances. The ability to comment would be extended to counsel for the prosecution as well as the judge, and it is hinted in the CLRC Report (although not stated in the draft Bill) that stronger comment from the judge would be permissible. Thus, under the CLRC proposal the suspect who is silent in interrogation would run the risk of having an inference drawn against him not only if he later raises a defence in court but also if he declines to give evidence.[6] The Home Office Working Group make a more limited proposal that the present power of the judge to comment on silence in court should be extended to the prosecution.[7]

The research sample contained no cases in which the defendant was silent in both the police station and court. However as noted above, the prospect of drawing an inference from silence would depend upon there being a case to answer. The early experience of implementing the reform of the right to silence in Northern Ireland was that courts were unwilling to draw inferences from silence where the positive evidence would have been insufficient to justify a conviction.[8] However, more recently the courts have used inferences drawn from silence to sustain convictions in circumstances where the positive evidence, taken alone, would have been insufficient[9]

Conclusion

The arguments for curtailing the right to silence are fundamentally utilitarian, promising that reform would bring advantages in terms of the more effective prosecution and conviction of offenders. These arguments are based on certain assumptions about the present workings of the criminal justice system and predictions about the likely effects of the reforms proposed. The limited purpose of the present research has been to test those assumptions and in the light of that to examine predictions about the likely effects of reform. The picture which emerges suggests that the right to silence is rarely exercised and that about half of those who exercise it are convicted. For cases which fail, there is little evidence to suggest that the prospects for conviction would be enhanced by inducing the suspect to speak or by treating his silence as evidence against him. In particular, the supposed benefits of interrogation – the opportunity to break down the suspect's defence or refute it by further investigation – accrue in only a small minority of cases. The extent of concern about

---

[6] Criminal Law Revision Committee Eleventh Report (1972) *Draft Criminal Evidence Bill* appended to the Report, cl 5.
[7] Home Office Working Group on the Right of Silence, Report (1989) 54.
[8] Ruddell (1990), P. 53.
[9] Jackson, (1991); Jackson, (1992).

ambush defences also appears to be misplaced. There is evidence to suggest that in a small number of cases in which the prosecution is faced with an unexpected defence, the root cause is failure by the police to allow a suspect to explain his proposed defence in interview. True ambush defences are very rare and may not always succeed when raised.

On the basis of these findings it can be anticipated that reform of the right to silence as proposed by the CLRC or Home Office Working Group would have a limited effect in enhancing the prospects of convicting guilty offenders in only a very small proportion of cases.

References

Baldwin, J. (1985). *Pre-trial justice.* Oxford: Basil Blackwell.

Baldwin, J. (1992). *The role of legal representatives at police stations.* A report prepared for the Royal Commission on Criminal Justice.

Baldwin, J. and McConville, M. (1980). *Confessions in Crown Court trials.* Royal Commission on Criminal Procedure Research Study, No. 5. London: HMSO.

Brown, D. (1989). *Detention at the police station under the Police and Criminal Evidence Act 1984.* Home Office Research Study No. 104. London: HMSO.

Criminal Law Revision Committee. (1972). *Eleventh Report, Evidence.* Cmnd. 4991. London: HMSO.

Cross, R. (1973). 'The evidence report: sense or nonsense?' *Criminal Law Review* 329.

Dixon, D. (1990). 'Politics, research and symbolism in criminal justice: the right to silence and the Police and Criminal Evidence Act'. *Anglo-American Law Review* 20, p.27.

Easton, S. (1991) *The right to silence.* Aldershot: Avebury.

Gobert, J. (1989). 'The peremptory challenge: an obituary'. *Criminal Law Review*, p. 528.

Greer, S. (1990). 'The right to silence: a review of the current debate'. *Modern Law Review*, 53, p.79.

Home Office (1989). *Report of the Working Group on the Right to Silence.*

Irving, B. (1980). *Police interrogation: a case study of current practice.* Royal Commission on Criminal Procedure Research Study No. 2. London: HMSO.

Irving, B. and Hilgendorf, L. (1980). *Police interrogation. The psychological approach.* Royal Commission on Criminal Procedure Research Study No. 1. London: HMSO.

Irving, B. and McKenzie, I. (1989). *Police interrogation: the effects of the Police and Criminal Evidence Act 1984.* London: Police Foundation.

Jackson, J. (1990). 'Recent developments in Northern Ireland'. In Greer, S. and Morgan, R. *The right to silence debate*, 44–52. Bristol and Bath Centre for Criminal Justice.

Jackson, J. (1991). 'Curtailing the right of silence: lessons from Northern Ireland'. *Criminal Law Review,* 404–415.

Jackson, J. (1992). 'The right of silence in Northern Ireland'. Paper given at the Civil Liberty Panel on Criminal Justice, 10 July 1992, the Inner Temple, London.

Lawton, F. (1987). 'How the right to silence has blocked convictions'. *The Independent,* 28 August.

McConville, M., Sanders, A., and Leng, R. (1991) *The case for the prosecution.* London: Routledge.

McConville, M. and Hodgson, J. (1992). *Custodial legal advice and the right to silence.* Report prepared for the Royal Commission on Criminal Justice.

McConville, M. (1992). *Corroboration and confessions: the impact of a rule requiring that no conviction can be sustained on the basis of confession evidence alone.* Report prepared for the Royal Commission on Criminal Justice.

McKenzie, I. and Irving, B. (1988). 'The right to silence' *Policing,* 4, p. 88.

Maguire, M. (1988) 'Effects of the PACE provisions on detention and questioning'. *British Journal of Criminology,* 28, p. 19.

Mark, R. (1973) *Minority verdict.* London: BBC publications.

Miller, C.J. (1973). 'Silence and confessions: what are they worth?' *Criminal Law Review* p.343.

Mitchell, B. (1983). 'Confessions and police interrogation of suspects'. *Criminal Law Review* p.596.

Moston, S., Stephenson, G. and Williamson T. (1992A). 'The effects of case characteristics on suspect behaviour during questioning'. *British Journal of Criminology,* 32, p. 23.

Moston, S., Stephenson, G. and Williamson T. (1992B). 'The incidence, antecedents and consequences of the use of the right to silence during police questioning'. Forthcoming *Criminal Behaviour and Mental Health.*

Royal Commission on Criminal Procedure. (1981A). *Report.* Cmnd 8092. London: HMSO.

Royal Commission on Criminal Procedure. (1981B) *The investigation and prosecution of criminal offences in England and Wales: the law and procedure.* Cmnd 8092. London: HMSO.

Ruddell, G. (1990). 'A summary of recent judicial decisions in Northern Ireland'. In Greer, S. and Morgan, R. *The right to silence debate*, 53–59. Bristol and Bath Centre for Criminal Justice.

Sanders, A. (1988). 'Rights, remedies and the Police and Criminal Evidence Act'. *Criminal Law Review*, p. 802.

Sanders, A. and Bridges, L. (1990). 'Access to legal advice and police malpractice'. *Criminal Law Review* 494.

Sanders, A., Bridges, L., Mulvaney, A., and Crozier, G. (1989). *Advice and assistance at police stations and the 24 hour duty solicitor scheme.* London: Lord Chancellor's Department.

Tapper, C. (1990). *Cross on Evidence* 7th edition. London: Butterworths.

Williams, G. (1987). 'The tactic of silence.' *New Law Journal*, 137, p. 1107.

Willis, C., McLeod, J. and Naish, P. (1988). *The tape-recording of interviews with suspects: a second interim report.* Home Office research Study No. 97. London: HMSO.

Zander, M. (1979). 'The investigation of crime: a study of cases tried at the Old Bailey'. *Criminal Law Review* p. 203.

Printed in the United Kingdom for HMSO.
Dd.0297210, 1/93, C6, 3396/4, 5673, 222863.